LOOKING for a CITY

Also by Roy Adams

Crossing Jordan
The Sanctuary
The Wonder of Jesus

BRIEFINGS FOR PILGRIMS ON THEIR JOURNEY HOME

LOOKING for a CITY

ROY ADAMS

REVIEW AND HERALD® PUBLISHING ASSOCIATION
Since 1861 | www.reviewandherald.com

Published by Review and Herald® Publishing Association, Hagerstown, MD 21741-1119

Review and Herald® titles may be purchased in bulk for educational, business, fund-raising, or sales promotional use. For information, e-mail SpecialMarkets@reviewandherald.com.

The Review and Herald® Publishing Association publishes biblically based materials for spiritual, physical, and mental growth and Christian discipleship.

This book was
Edited by Vesna Mirkovich
Copyedited by Delma Miller
Cover design by Emily Ford/Review and Herald® Design Center
Cover art © Thinkstock.com
Interior design by Derek Knecht/Review and Herald® Design Center
Typeset: Minion Pro 11/13

PRINTED IN U.S.A.

18 17 16 15 14 5 4 3 2 1

Library of Congress Cataloging-in-Publication Data
Adams, Roy, 1941-
Looking for a city : briefings for pilgrims on their journey home / Roy Adams.
pages cm
Includes bibliographical references and index.
ISBN 978-0-8280-2701-4 (alk. paper)
1. Seventh-Day Adventists--Doctrines. 2. Christian life--Seventh-day Adventist authors. I. Title.
BX6154.A5625 2014
230'.6732--dc23

2013002964

ISBN 978-0-8280-2701-4

Dedication

For my wife, Celia,
and our children, Dwayne and Kim

And for my sisters,
Maudlyn, Flossie, and Claradell,
and my brothers, Dennis and Husford

Acknowledgments

Over the decades, as I worked as a pastor, a teacher, an editor, and in other capacities, it was my privilege to interact with a multitude of Seventh-day Adventist Christians, as well as Christians of other faith traditions. I've participated in hundreds of discussion groups and forums, and my speaking appointments have taken me literally around the world.

Through it all, I've tried both to speak and to listen. And much of what I've learned from others is reflected in the pages of this book. I want to acknowledge my indebtedness to this vast, nameless, but vital group of agents in my life and ministry. And especially to those who interacted with me during my time with the *Adventist Review/Adventist World* magazines, and whose letters, e-mails, phone calls, and prayers have encouraged and strengthened me in my work.

I would also express my gratitude for the encouragement I received from the Review and Herald acquisitions editor Jeannette Johnson and vice president for editorial services Dwain Esmond upon submission of the manuscript for this book and during the acceptance process. Vesna Mirkovich took on the tedious task of editing the document, in a couple of cases even tracking down a footnote or two that had eluded me. My thanks, too, to Delma Miller for her copyediting work, always a painstaking task.

Above all, I give thanks to God, who continues to provide the urge to write and the strength to do it.

Contents

Preface

I write to get things off my chest: things I feel compelled to share, things I hope will make a difference. The chapters in this book came together as separate units and as such do not present a running story line. Each one stands complete, which means that each could serve as an appropriate entry point into the book.

Notwithstanding the unconnected nature of the chapters, they fall under four overarching themes. Chapters 2 and 3 belong under *protology*, the study of how things began. Few other areas of human knowledge have a greater potential to influence our personal lives, our behavior, and our sense of worth. Chapters 4 and 5 fall in the area of *soteriology*, the doctrine of salvation. They highlight the inscrutable love of God and what theologians refer to as God's scandalous grace.

Chapters 6 to 12 comprise the third theme, *living in the world*, and focus on a wide range of issues dealing with the Christian struggle, with the ongoing challenge of living godly in increasingly hostile spiritual environments. And two chapters under this theme (10 and 11) touch on the vital importance of rest and worship in building Christian community and solidarity, as well as enhancing personal spiritual growth.

The final theme, *eschatology* (the doctrine of last-day issues and events), occupies chapters 13 to 18. During the course of my ministerial career I've preached few sermons that did not end with the subject of the second coming of Jesus. It's part of the warp and woof of who I am as an Adventist Christian. I genuinely want to see this Person from whom I've received nothing but kindness. But as you will see, I do not follow the customary Jesus-is-coming-soon approach. Rather, I grapple with the issues and implications of the Advent from the standpoint of our particular place in history.

But if eschatology ends the book, it also begins it, the first and last chapters working in tandem and forming an envelope, as it were, for the rest of the work. In other words, the book ends where it begins—with the bubbling Christian hope of the hereafter. The very title of that first chapter ("One Hundred Billion Stanzas") gets my blood pumping when I remember where it happens—the sea of glass before the throne of God. My hope is that everyone will read that chapter first. Straddling all the materials in between, it connects with the last chapter, whose title ("Looking for a City") harps back to Hebrews, where it says of Abraham that "he was looking forward to the city with foundations, whose architect and builder is God" (Heb. 11:10).

I see these 18 chapters as mere *splashes of grace* on God's great cosmic canvas. Yet preparing them has drawn me closer to His love. And my prayer is that reading them may do the same for you.

Chapter 1

One Hundred Billion Stanzas . . . and a Single Chorus

I saw in heaven another great and marvelous sign: seven angels with the seven last plagues—last, because with them God's wrath is completed. And I saw what looked like a sea of glass glowing with fire and, standing beside the sea, those who had been victorious over the beast and its image and over the number of its name. They held harps given them by God and sang the song of God's servant Moses the servant of God and of the Lamb: 'Great and marvelous are your deeds, Lord God Almighty. Just and true are your ways, King of the nations'" (Rev. 15:1-3).

The above passage, as I see it, speaks about three things: (1) a God who's had it, (2) a people who've made it, and (3) a song that proclaims it.

A God Who's Had It

I sometimes feel my chest burning with frustration and outrage as I watch the evening news. The injustice, the exploitation, the senseless violence, the ghastly killing of innocent people by rogues dressed up as leaders. In the recent past the sordid underbelly of corrupt humanity has been on full display: the sexual trafficking in human beings, whereby criminals wreck the lives of countless women, girls, and boys; the willful manipulation of national economies by unscrupulous parasites, secreting away billions of dollars and putting millions of individuals in financial peril; the deadly trade in illicit drugs, with its resulting mayhem and brutality (as in Mexico, where in the latter part of the previous decade 40,000 people were killed in drug-related violence); the brutal physical dismemberment of fellow human beings by cold-blooded insurgents; the specter of genocide in multiple places around the world.

Add to all this society's steady descent into immorality. Today we're using some of the most advanced technological wizardry in the history of humanity to debase and corrupt one another with every imaginable form of decadence that sick minds can devise. The on-screen carnage in popular entertainment—some of it in slow motion for greater, mind-numbing effect, allowing us to experience the mayhem, the gore, the sharp knife plunging into living flesh, the human brain blown apart with a high-powered gun. The result we're seeing is the brutalization of an entire generation. We're producing a brood of sophisticated savages, without morals or values or conscience.

Then there's the perennial human perversity—exponentially exacerbated in our times—that attempts to expel God from His own universe. I still remember the week *Time* magazine came out with its provocative cover billboard—big red letters against a jet-black background: "IS GOD DEAD?"[1] Those were the heady days of the 1960s and 1970s, when affluent, well-fed Western theologians strutted their sacrilegious stuff for all to see. Those were the days when British theologian and rising star John A. T. Robinson (citing his compatriot biologist Julian Huxley) suggested that "the god hypothesis . . . [was] no longer of any pragmatic value for the interpretation . . . of nature." "Operationally," he said, "God is beginning to resemble not a ruler but the last fading smile of a cosmic Cheshire Cat."[2]

Perhaps not with the same degree of cockiness, but with no less disdain, the trend continues today. In his 2007 book *God Is Not Great* journalist Christopher Hitchens spoke about "the stupid notion of 'intelligent design.'"[3] According to him, we needn't posit the existence of God as an explanation for the universe.

And in a January 13, 2012, interview with Ira Flatow on National Public Radio's *Science Friday,* Lawrence Krauss, director of the Origins Project at Arizona State University, repeated sentiments he'd already expressed in his book *A Universe From Nothing:*[4] "We don't yet know the true origin of life," he said, "but we think we'll understand it by chemistry, and what we're discovering is that in fact physics has suggested that maybe the same is true for the whole universe, that we don't need a creator."[5] I saw a promotional blurb for Krauss's book on Amazon.com (which probably will have disappeared by the time you read this) describing Krauss's book as "a fascinating antidote to outmoded philosophical and religious thinking, . . . a provocative, game-changing entry into the debate about the existence of God and everything that exists. 'Forget Jesus,' Krauss has argued, 'the stars died so you could be born.'"[6]

God has placed us in a mind-boggling universe. But our venture into its intriguing mysteries, instead of making us humble and teachable and absolutely awestruck with astonishment and wonder, seems to make us cockier, more presumptuous, more arrogant. We look up into the mind-blowing heavens *and have the audacity (not to mention the stupidity)* to suggest that it all came about from some accidental big bang!

Brings to mind the words of Shakespeare: "O judgment, thou art fled to brutish beasts, and men have lost their reason!"[7]

And here's how God features in the picture I've been painting: after the likes of me have read the papers, watched the evening news, taken in just a tiny fraction of the outrageous goings-on in the world, and gone to bed, God remains awake. He sees it all, hears it all, knows it all—every nook and cranny of this wretched planet. He's been patient, "compassionate and gracious . . . slow to anger, abounding in love and faithfulness" (Ex. 34:6). But as biblical history shows, that patience is not unlimited. And Revelation 15:1 *reveals a God who's had it.* His phenomenal forbearance with our sacrilegious insubordination has run its lengthy course, and seven angels, "the seven last plagues" in their hands, stand poised to pour out His fury upon a rebellious planet.

However patient, God can bear no more. He's had it *up to here*!

A People Who've Made It!

In the vision John saw "standing [*on*] the sea"[8] of glass "those who had been victorious over the beast and its image and over the number of its name" (Rev. 15:2).

In other words, *they've made it*!

Just think what that means. No other aspiration could be more important or critical for the Christian than making it onto that resplendent sea before the throne of God. But perhaps there's no Christian, fully aware of his or her own fickleness, who has never, in the dead of night, experienced a certain dread about not getting there.

About two to three months after we students had done the Higher Senior Cambridge (HSC) exams under the British education system, the headmaster of the school would drive down to the post office when the exam results had arrived back from the United Kingdom (where they were graded). Keen watchers of the headmaster's movements around results time, we waited breathless for his return. With a large brown legal-size envelope in his hand, he'd walk to the front of the class, pull out the alphabetized list of those who'd made it, and commence reading. We all sat there petrified, hearts pounding as loud as jackhammers. If he got to the B names and I didn't hear Adams, that would mean I had failed. And failure meant taking your desk right then and there (that was the tradition) and carrying it back to the classroom across the campus, from which you'd been provisionally promoted, in full view of the entire school—an exceedingly humiliating event for those who did not make it.

Yet making it onto the Cambridge list is nothing compared to whether your name—my name—gets read out "when the roll is called up yonder." And the passage before us points out the formidable impediments in our path. Those who make it onto that dazzling sea, it says, will have been "victorious over the beast and its image and over the number of its name." In other words, those who make it there will have done so in the face of unimaginable social and religious pressure to compromise, to conform, to abandon their faith in Jesus. Like Christian in John Bunyan's *Pilgrim's Progress,* they will have run the gauntlet of a thousand obstacles—from the Slough of Despond to the Enchanted Ground to Doubting Castle and the Valley of Death.

In Homer's celebrated legend *The Odyssey*, one deadly peril after another confronts Odysseus and his men on their journey home: the hazardous crossing between the lethal monsters Scylla and Charybdis; the frightening encounter with Cyclops, the terrible one-eyed giant; and perhaps worst of all, the wickedly enchanting music of the Sirens from their perch atop the bones of hapless sailors who, beguiled by their treacherous melodies, had ventured ashore to check them out.

Like Christian and Odysseus, we face a host of frightening perils on our journey home. But there's hope. Revelation 17:14 speaks of an amalgam of evil powers in the last days making "war with the Lamb." But, it says, "the Lamb will overcome them, for He is Lord of lords and King of kings; and those who are with Him are called, chosen, and faithful" (NKJV). Earlier John saw them "standing before the throne and before the Lamb, clothed with white robes" (Rev. 7:9, NKJV). They'd come "out of the great tribulation" and had "washed their robes . . . in the blood of the Lamb" (verse 14, NKJV).

They'd made it—through the blood of Jesus!

Our anxieties will vanish when we understand that the battle is not ours, but God's. The Lamb will fight for us. And for all who worry about not making it, Ellen G. White has these encouraging words: "The message from God to me for you is 'Him that cometh unto me, I will in no wise cast out' (John 6:37). If you have nothing else to plead before God but this one promise from your Lord and Savior, you have the assurance that you will never, never be turned away." She reiterates with continued emphasis, "It may seem to you that you are hanging upon a single promise, but appropriate that one promise, and it will open to you the whole treasure house of the riches of the grace of Christ. Cling to that promise and you are safe. . . . Present this assurance to Jesus, and you are as safe as though inside the city of God."[9]

We can make it! And by God's grace, we will.

A Song That Proclaims It

Moses and the Israelites had only just left Egypt when Pharaoh, suddenly realizing the immense loss of free labor their departure represented, changed his mind. When the Israelites looked back, what they saw bearing down upon them was the full military hardware of the most powerful nation on earth. Prevented by the terrain from turning either right or left, the only remaining option was the sea.

Impossible!

They felt cornered, trapped. Desperate, they cried to God for help. And the divine response, stranger than the wildest fiction: "Tell the Israelites to go forward" (Ex. 14:15, NRSV). Toward the open sea!

Today we know the outcome, but at that moment they didn't!

The astounding, hair-raising spectacle—when it was over—brought to Moses' mind a new song, a song of deliverance that includes the words "I will sing to the Lord, for he is highly exalted. Both horse and driver he has hurled into the sea. The Lord is my strength and my defense; he has become my salvation. . . . The enemy boasted, . . . But you blew with your breath, and the sea covered them. They sank like lead in the mighty waters. Who among the gods is like you, Lord? Who is like you—majestic in holiness, awesome in glory, working wonders?" (Ex. 15:1-11).

Powerful as that song is, it remains the song of Moses, not the song of the Lamb. Indeed, the song of the Lamb is nowhere to be found in the Old Testament. And we can look in the New Testament from Matthew to Jude and not find it.

But there it is in the heart of the Apocalypse! And through the vision of the seer of Patmos, we already know its chorus, the chorus we'll be singing on that glorious day upon the sea of glass. "They held harps given them by God," John says, "and sang the song of God's servant Moses and of the Lamb: 'Great and marvelous are your deeds, Lord God Almighty. Just and true are your ways, King of the nations'" (Rev. 15:2, 3).

My wife and I were at the Kennedy Center in Washington, D.C., for a performance of Mendelssohn's "Music to a *Midsummer Night's Dream*." The orchestra moved through the various parts of the piece listed in the program—the Scherzo, the Melodrama, the March of the Fairies, the Nocturne, the Wedding March, the Funeral March, the Dance of the Clowns. Then as they came down toward the finale, two soloists from the University of Maryland Concert Choir joined in, their hauntingly beautiful voices evoking the enchanting strains of the Sirens of ancient Greek legend.

Other voices entered from other members of the choir. Then as the group came together, the complete choir combining full-throttle with the orchestra, goose bumps broke out all over my body! That evening, albeit in a purely secular setting, I got a *faint glimpse* of what will happen one day upon the sea of glass.

As I imagine it, the Song of Moses commences the celebrations, with Moses as the lead soloist, Aaron accompanying him in duets from time to time, other members of the Exodus party forming the massive choir, Miriam directing.

The drama heightens, with the theme of the music broadening beyond the Exodus event to the multifaceted experiences of God's people through all time. As the pace picks up, the angel Gabriel seamlessly taking the lead, the Song of Moses is embellished by a stanza from the life of Enoch—about his translation and his walk with God; by a stanza from the life of Noah, the great veteran of the Deluge; by a stanza from the life of Abraham, God's poster child for naked faith; a stanza from the life of Jacob—about how, in utter weakness and discouragement, he'd struggled with God and prevailed; a stanza from Rahab the prostitute; a stanza from Hannah the persistent suppliant; a stanza from Elijah, the dogged prophet; a stanza each from Isaiah, Jeremiah, Daniel, Jonah, Stephen, Peter, Paul, and John the revelator; stanzas from spiritual veterans and martyrs across the centuries; and, finally, stanzas from the likes of you and me, sharing highlights of our heartaches and our burdens, our hopes and fears, our anxieties and pain, about tear-drenched pillows in the midnight hour, and about how we made it over!

All over the sea of glass unending stanzas pop up among the vast multitude from every tribe and nation standing there before the throne of God—each stanza telling stories about how God helped us, led us, fed us, kept us, saved us. Anyone who's ever attended a testimony service and felt hot tears flow over the powerful intervention of God in the life of some burdened, suffering saint can anticipate a little of what it'll be like on the sea of glass.

As the Song of Moses, overwhelmed by 100 million stanzas[10] from saints and martyrs from all across the planet and through the centuries, swells into the song of the Lamb, Gabriel pulls out all the stops, raises the pitch a thousand octaves, and 100 million voices, in ear-splitting unison, fill the entire universe with one humongous anthem, whose *single,* exciting chorus we already know: "Great and marvelous are your deeds, Lord God Almighty. Just and true are your ways, King of the nations."

It's a song of joy—unadulterated joy; a song of praise—exuberant praise; a song of deliverance—ultimate deliverance; a song of victory—final, decisive, absolute. Golf-ball-size goose bumps break out on arms and faces all across the sea of glass! The sheer joy of it! To think that we're finally home! No more disappointment, no more pain, no more crying, no more death.

---

[1] *Time,* Apr. 8, 1966.

[2] Julian Huxley, *Religion Without Revelation,* 2nd ed., p. 58, cited in John A. T. Robinson, *Honest to God* (Philadelphia: Westminster Press, 1963), pp. 37, 38.

[3] Christopher Hitchens, *God Is Not Great* (New York: Twelve Hatchet Books, 2007), p. 85.

[4] Lawrence M. Krauss, *A Universe From Nothing: Why There Is Something Rather Than Nothing* (New York: Free Press, 2012).

[5] Lawrence M. Krauss on *A Universe From Nothing,* interview by Ira Flatow, *Talk of the Nation,* National Public Radio, Jan. 13, 2012, http://www.npr.org/2012/01/13/145175263/lawrence-krauss-on-a-universe-from-nothing.

[6] Book description of *A Universe From Nothing: Why There Is Something Rather Than Nothing,* by Lawrence M. Krauss, http://www.amazon.com/o/ASIN/145162445X/science-friday/.

[7] William Shakespeare, *Julius Caesar,* Act III, scene 2, lines 109, 110.

[8] "On" is undoubtedly the correct translation of the Greek *epi* here (rather than "beside"). Indeed, though *epi* occurs numerous other times in the book of Revelation, the New International Version (NIV) has chosen to translate it "beside" only here. The NIV's usual translation of the word is "on," as in Revelation 7:3; 9:4; 12:1, etc.

[9] Ellen G. White, *Manuscript Releases* (Silver Spring, Md.: Ellen G. White Estate, 1990), vol. 10, p. 175.

[10] The number here and in the title of the chapter assumes one stanza for every person saved. Of course, no one knows (or can know) the number of the saved. But Jesus indicated that the number of those lost will far exceed that of the saved (see Matt.

7:13, 14). According to the Population Reference Bureau's admittedly speculative estimate, some 108 billion people have lived on earth (Carl Haub, "How Many People Have Lived on Earth?" Population Reference Bureau, www.prb.org/Articles/2002/HowManyPeopleHaveEverLivedonEarth.aspx). But since Jesus indicated that the number of those lost will far exceed that of the saved (see Matt. 7:13, 14), the expression "100 billion stanzas" used in this chapter assumes that many of the redeemed will be bubbling over with many more than a single stanza.

Chapter 2

Atheists Going for the Jugular . . . and Religion Fighting Back

When I made a passing reference to British atheist Richard Dawkins during a sermon at an Alberta, Canada, camp meeting back in 2008 (taking all of 10 seconds to do it), I never expected the name to register with anyone in the audience. So I was surprised when, following the service, a young woman approached me about my remarks.

"There's a guy down in my office—a friend of mine," she said. "He's reading Dawkins and is very impressed. Do you know of anyone who has answered him, any book I might recommend?"

"Alister McGrath," I said as she wrote it down. "The name of his book is *The Dawkins Delusion?*" (And the book's subtitle, which I couldn't remember at the time, is *Atheist Fundamentalism and the Denial of the Divine.*)[1] McGrath, an atheist-turned-Christian, received a doctorate in molecular biophysics at Oxford, and his book presents a masterful response to Dawkins. This chapter focuses on McGrath's response to Dawkins, with my own (lay) critique thrown in. The initial idea for this exposé came when I heard McGrath deliver a powerful rejoinder to Dawkins at a conference I attended in Cambridge, England, in April 2007.

So what is Dawkins about?

Spewing Venom

The title of Dawkins' book *The God Delusion* says it all—no subtitle needed.[2] And right from the start, in the preface, he puts his cards out on the table for all to see: "If this book works as I intend, religious readers who open it will be atheists when they put it down."[3]

That cocky prediction makes one shudder just a little. *What faith-shattering stuff am I in for?* But then, as if bracing himself for a less-than-total knockout in every instance, Dawkins throws a (derisive) caveat into the mix. "Of course," he says, "dyed-in-the-wool faith-heads are immune to argument, their resistance built up over years of childhood indoctrination."[4]

Getting down to business in chapter 2, this Oxford science professor moves quickly to his major target. "The God of the Old Testament," he says, "is arguably the most unpleasant character in all fiction [the words are loaded]: jealous and proud of it; a petty, unjust, unforgiving control-freak; a vindictive, bloodthirsty ethnic cleanser; a misogynistic, homophobic, racist, infanticidal, genocidal, filicidal, pestilential, megalomaniacal, sadomasochistic, capriciously malevolent bully."[5]

As Dawkins sees it, much of the world's problems come from our blindly following this and other capricious gods—figments of the human mind. So with John Lennon of Beatles' fame, he dares to dream of "a world with no religion." It would be a place with "no suicide bombers, no 9/11, . . . no Crusades, no witch-hunts, . . . no Israeli/Palestinian wars, no Serb/Croat/Muslim massacres, no persecution of Jews as 'Christ-killers.'"[6] (He conveniently ignores the massacres of untold millions by such atheists as Adolf Hitler and Joseph Stalin.)

Intelligent people don't dabble with religion, Dawkins says—and especially not scientists! "Great scientists who profess religion . . . stand out for their rarity," he says, "and are a subject of amused bafflement to their peers in the academic community." He once asked Jim Watson (whom he describes as the "founding genius of the Human Genome Project") "whether he knew many religious scientists today." According to Dawkins, Watson replied, "Virtually none."[7]

In response to this claim, however, McGrath notes that in 2006, the very year *The God Delusion* was published, "Owen Gingerich, a noted Harvard astronomer, produced *God's Universe*, declaring that 'the universe has been created with intention and purpose, and that this belief does not interfere with the scientific enterprise.'" McGrath also points out that in that same year "Francis Collins published his *Language of God*, which argues that the wonder and ordering of nature points to a Creator God, very much along the lines of traditional Christian conception."[8] And that same year too, "cosmologist Paul Davies published his *Goldilocks Enigma*, arguing for the existence of 'fine-tuning' in the universe."[9]

"Underlying the agenda of *The God Delusion*," says McGrath, is that "atheism is the only option for the serious, progressive, thinking person," and that religious experience is "associated with pathological brain activity."[10] The gospel, Dawkins says, is fiction.[11] And as if appealing to the coming generation still making up its mind, Dawkins proffers something akin to spiritual assurance: "You can be an atheist who is happy, balanced, moral, and intellectually fulfilled."[12]

It's a conscious, calculated effort on Dawkins' part—an "epic struggle against religion," McGrath calls it.[13] Dawkins sees science and religion as "locked in a battle to the death. Only one can emerge victorious—and it must be science."[14] Dawkins' goal is "the intellectual and cultural destruction of religion," says McGrath.[15] He thrusts to kill. He goes for the jugular.

Dawkins' Achilles' Heel

The chapter "Why There Almost Certainly Is No God" is probably the pivotal section of Dawkins' book. And in the first of a six-point summary of that chapter's content, Dawkins captures perhaps the central issue of the book: "One of the greatest challenges to the human intellect, over the centuries, has been to explain *how the complex, improbable appearance of design in the universe arises*."[16]

How would Dawkins deal with this fundamental issue of having to explain the apparent element of design in the universe?

In this connection, two creationist arguments concerned him: (1) the argument from improbability and (2) the argument from irreducible complexity.

Improbability

Simply put, the argument from improbability suggests that the complexity we see within and around us demands that there be a superior intelligence behind it. Or to paraphrase the way Dawkins himself characterized it (quoting Fred Hoyle), the probability of life originating on earth by itself is tantamount to "the chance that a hurricane, sweeping through a scrapyard, would have the luck to assemble a Boeing 747."[17]

But however apparently convincing, says Dawkins, such arguments are made only by those who know nothing about natural selection.[18] Citing Daniel Dennett, whom he adores as a "scientifically savvy philosopher," Dawkins argues that it does not take "a big fancy smart thing to make a lesser thing." The uninitiated would attempt to make their case for intelligent design by suggesting that "you'll never see a horseshoe making a blacksmith" or "a pot making a potter." But, says Dawkins confidently, "*Darwin's discovery of a workable process that does that very counterintuitive thing is what makes his contribution to human thought so revolutionary*."[19]

What Dawkins advocates here is that however counterintuitive, *horseshoes do, indeed, make blacksmiths!*

Incredible!

And how does that happen? Not by chance (Dawkins hates that word), but by natural selection.[20] "Natural selection," Dawkins says, "is the champion crane of all time. It has lifted life from primeval simplicity to the dizzy heights of complexity, beauty and apparent design that dazzle us today."[21] The upshot of his argument is that since natural selection is responsible for all we see around us, "God . . . is a delusion."[22]

Such logic boggles the mind and calls on people to abandon fundamental common sense. It's the kind of thinking that led MIT-trained physicist and biologist Gerald L. Schroeder to make the following incisive comment, which came after he'd grappled with the fantastic working of the nerves and the human brain: "Knowing the complexity of the processes involved," he says, "when we see a diagram showing how simple evolution is, how one organ can change into another merely by adding a feature here and there, we must realize that those demonstrations are a farce."

"As long as the intricate workings of the cell are disregarded," Schroeder continues, "there's no problem for a Steven Pinker, or Stephen Jay Gould, or Richard Dawkins to talk of random reactions producing the goods of life." Then, as if smarting from the weight that such scientific charlatans nevertheless carry among certain intellectuals today, Schroeder wraps up by saying: "It is hard not to be fooled by the foolish arguments when they originate from intelligent foolers."[23]

Words to ponder.

Irreducible Complexity

Popularized by Michael J. Behe in *Darwin's Black Box*, irreducible complexity suggests that the life forms we know today—even the simplest ones—comprise interlocking, interdependent components, too complex to have evolved individually through chance or natural selection.[24] In this connection, Darwin himself pointed to the eye as posing a particularly challenging problem, and Dawkins repeats the master's words in his book. Darwin said, "To suppose that the eye with all its inimitable contrivances for adjusting the focus to different distances, for admitting different amounts of light, and for the correction of spherical and chromatic aberration, could have been formed by natural selection, seems, I freely confess, absurd in the highest degree."[25]

It's a cogent observation indeed. But Darwin (with Dawkins following) would find a way around it. Darwin's statement, according to Dawkins, was merely a "rhetorical device" to lure his opponents closer to him so he could administer a more powerful punch. And that punch, says Dawkins, "was Darwin's effortless explanation of exactly how the eye evolved by gradual degrees."[26]

In *The God Delusion* Dawkins explains such a feat by recounting a parable he had used in an earlier book, *Climbing Mount Improbable* (1966).[27] He imagines a mountain with a sheer cliff on one side, "impossible to climb, but on the other side is a gentle slope to the summit. On the summit," he further imagines, "sits a complex device such as an eye." We should not imagine, as do intelligent design proponents, that such complexity "could spontaneously self-assemble." That, he says, would be an "absurd notion," for it would be like "leaping from the foot of the cliff to the top in one bound."[28] Evolution, rather, does it the proper way, he says. It "goes around the back of the mountain and creeps up the gentle slope to the summit: easy!"[29]

So the picture Dawkins draws here is that of a vast quantity of primordial materials (as if we knew where such things might come from!) slowly ascending "Mount Improbable," each particular unit at some point arriving at the maximum state of complexity and then somehow linking up with other complexities to form discrete, living, functioning entities!

Perhaps himself impressed by the fantasy of it all, Dawkins says that "if genuinely irreducible complexity could be properly demonstrated, *it would wreck Darwin's theory*."[30] But irreducible complexity needs no demonstration; it's reality. And it's difficult to see why anyone would substitute Dawkins' irrational speculation for the simple dignity of the biblical affirmation "In the beginning God created" (Gen. 1:1).

Where I Come Down

The contemporary period has seen a spate of attacks on God, the Bible, and all things religious in works such as Daniel C. Dennett's *Breaking the Spell: Religion as a Natural Phenomenon* (2006), David Mills' *Atheist Universe: The Thinking Person's Answer to Christian Fundamentalism* (2006), and Christopher Hitchens' *God Is Not Great: How Religion Poisons Everything* (2007). As I rode a bus in Chicago one November day in 2008, I fell into conversation with a fellow conference attendee who, before we parted, handed me a flyer for a book by Bob Avakian entitled *Away With All Gods!: Unchaining the Mind and Radically Changing the World*.

We're facing a veritable anti-God epidemic, much of it related to pseudoscientific philosophy. And it would be easy for us to vacate the field, curling our tails between our legs like frightened dogs. After all, many of us (myself first) are not scientists and, if you're like me, are hesitant to enter the gated scientific community without permission. Yet as freethinking human beings we have a right to stand up against atheistic fundamentalism, every bit as intolerant as its religious counterpart.

Dawkins represents that kind of intolerance. McGrath, himself a scientist, describes Dawkins as offering "the atheistic equivalent of slick hellfire preaching, substituting turbocharged rhetoric and highly selective manipulation of facts for careful, evidence-based thinking." McGrath suggests that it's an abuse of the natural sciences in the interest of atheist fundamentalism.[31]

Two points to finish: First, like McGrath, I'm not impressed by Dawkins' selective references to religious institutions and people to make his point. "There is . . . a lunatic fringe to every movement," McGrath suggests. "[And] one of the most characteristic features of Dawkins' antireligious polemic is to present the pathological as if it were normal, the fringe as if it were the center, crackpots as if they were mainstream."[32]

Still, I find it beyond unfortunate that Christians, of all religious people, should have provided Dawkins and other atheists so much grist for their mills. When Dawkins maligns the religious education of children, for example, he is able to point convincingly to flagrant abuses of children committed within Christian religious educational settings. Shame on us!

Second, Nobel Prize-winning Oxford immunologist Peter Medawar has made the point that there are questions at once "elementary" and "transcendent" that "science cannot answer, and that no conceivable advance of science would empower it to answer," namely, questions such as "How did everything begin? What are we all here for? What is the point of living?"[33]

Such questions have to do with protology and eschatology. Protology, the study of origins (how we got here, etc.), occupied us briefly under the previous section, "Dawkins' Achilles' Heel." And we saw a little of Dawkins' tortured attempt to grapple with it. Here we note the bleakness of his eschatology—what he himself calls "the ultimate fate of our universe." "Depending upon the values [of certain numbers]," he says, "our universe may be destined to expand indefinitely, or it may stabilize at an equilibrium, or the expansion may reverse itself and go into contraction, culminating in the so-called 'big crunch.' "[34]

What a bleak picture! Bleaker still when put in the words of Bertrand Russell, one of Dawkins' philosophical mentors. Russell envisioned that "all the labors of the ages, all the devotion, all the inspiration, all the noonday brightness of human genius, are destined to extinction in the vast death of the solar system."[35]

Why would one accept that dismal prospect in place of what the Bible offers? Here it is, in all its elegance, from the seer of Patmos:

"I saw Heaven and earth new-created. Gone the first Heaven, gone the first earth, gone the sea. I saw Holy Jerusalem, new-created, descending resplendent out of Heaven, as ready for God as a bride for her husband. I heard a voice thunder from the Throne: 'Look! Look! God has moved into the neighborhood, making his home with men and women! . . . He'll wipe every tear from their eyes. Death is gone for good—tears gone, crying gone, pain gone. . . .' The Enthroned continued, 'Look! I'm making everything new. Write it all down—each word dependable and accurate' " (Rev. 21:1-5, Message).

It doesn't get any better!

---

[1] Alister E. and Joanna Collicutt McGrath, *The Dawkins Delusion?* (Downers Grove, Ill.: IVP Books, 2007). Notwithstanding the book's coauthorship, all future references to authorship in this chapter will be to Alister McGrath, as if he were the sole author, a procedure they themselves follow in the book.

[2] Richard Dawkins, *The God Delusion* (Boston: Houghton Mifflin Co., 2006).

[3] Dawkins, p. 28.

[4] *Ibid.*

[5] *Ibid.*, p. 51.

[6] *Ibid.*, pp. 23, 24.

[7] *Ibid.*, p. 125.

[8] McGrath, p. 42. However, see chapter 3, which assesses Francis Collins' position on a broader scope.

[9] *Ibid.*

[10] *Ibid.*, pp. 33, 66.

[11] Dawkins, p. 123.

[12] *Ibid.*, p. 23.

[13] McGrath, p. 51.

[14] *Ibid.*, p. 46.

[15] *Ibid.*, p. 24.

[16] Dawkins, p. 188. (Italics supplied.)

[17] *Ibid.*, pp. 137, 138.

[18] *Ibid.*, p. 138.

[19] *Ibid*., p. 142. (Italics supplied.)
[20] *Ibid.*
[21] *Ibid*., p. 99.
[22] *Ibid*., p. 52.
[23] Gerald L. Schroeder, *The Hidden Face of God: How Science Reveals the Ultimate Truth* (New York: Free Press, 2001), p. 103.
[24] Michael J. Behe, *Darwin's Black Box: The Biochemical Challenge to Evolution* (New York: Free Press, 1996, 2006).
[25] Quoted in Dawkins, pp. 148, 149.
[26] *Ibid*., p. 149.
[27] Note, however, that I am citing the parable as Dawkins retells it in *The God Delusion*, p. 147.
[28] *Ibid.* Incidentally, proponents of intelligent design do not suggest that complexity "could spontaneously self-assemble," as Dawkins suggests, but rather that some intelligent mind had to have been responsible for that assemblage.
[29] *Ibid.*
[30] *Ibid*., p. 151. (Italics supplied.)
[31] McGrath, p. 11.
[32] *Ibid*., p. 22.
[33] Peter Medawar, *Advice to a Young Scientist* (London: Harper & Row, 1979), p. 31. Cf. http://hyperphysics.phy-astr.gsu.edu/nave-html/faithpathh/Medawar.html; McGrath, p. 39.
[34] Dawkins, p. 174.
[35] Bertrand Russell, "A Free Man's Worship," The Bertrand Russell Society, http://users.drew.edu/~jlenz/br-fmw.html. This Web site cites the source *Mysticism and Logic: and Other Essays* (Ithaca, N.Y.: Cornell University Library, 2009).

Chapter 3

Theistic Evolution: Brilliant Coup or Strategic Retreat?

Many Christians have come to accept evolution as the means through which all biological species came to be. But unable to stomach the idea of mechanistic evolution, some in this group prefer to go the way of "theistic evolution" ("theistic" coming from *theos,* the Greek word for *God*). In other words, they believe that God guided the process.

Especially in conservative Christian circles, however, those who advocate this notion tend to do so in whispers. Which is why I found it refreshing that Francis Collins would boldly unfurl his theistic evolution colors for all to see, in his book *The Language of God: A Scientist Presents Evidence for Belief.*[1]

In this chapter I use Collins' book as a convenient point of reference and offer four observations on Collins' position and on related issues of origins.

1. Collins' stance is a powerful testimony for faith.

Given Collins' high-profile scientific credentials, his conviction probably goes a long way in breaking the logjam between atheistic materialism and religion, at least for conflicted scientists looking for direction and religious scientists and others feeling shaky in their commitment to faith. Currently director of the National Institutes of Health (an agency of the United States Department of Health and Human Services and a leading center for medical research), Collins—a scientist and physician—served as head of the Human Genome Project (1993-2008), an international group of scientists laboring to map, for the first time, the complete sequence of the human DNA. The title of his book *(The Language of God)* is a takeoff on the project's dramatic, precedent-shattering breakthrough, and a deliberate attempt to cast God as the Mastermind behind the complex human design.

At a White House event celebrating the genome discovery, Collins was open about his convictions: "It is humbling for me, and awe-inspiring," he said, "to realize that we have caught the first glimpse of our own instruction book, previously known only to God. . . . For me," Collins went on, "the experience of sequencing the human genome, and uncovering this most remarkable of all texts, was both a stunning scientific achievement and an occasion of worship"[2]

In the book Collins seeks to dispel the notion "that a rigorous scientist could not also be a serious believer in a transcendent God." For him, "belief in God can be an entirely rational choice, . . . and . . . the principles of faith are . . . complementary with the principles of science."[3] Such sentiments are a far cry from those of scientists such as Richard Dawkins, who at the end of chapter 4 of one of his books boldly asserts that "if the argument of this chapter is accepted, the factual premise of religion—the God Hypothesis—is untenable. God almost certainly does not exist."[4]

But just as Bible-believing Christians begin to get comfortable with Collins, they come in for a rude awakening, as quickly becomes evident.

2. Often the most logical faith statements get savaged, while palpably outlandish "scientific" pronouncements go unchallenged.

In his 1802 book, *Natural Theology,* for example, William Paley came up with his famous watchmaker analogy. Basically, he argued that an ordinary person finding a watch in an open field would logically conclude that such a complex machine could not have happened by accident but rather had to have had an intelligent designer. It's a commonsense inference; but, surprisingly, it does not fly with Collins.

The point Paley is making, says Collins, "can be summarized as follows:

1. "A watch is complex.
2. "A watch has an intelligent designer.
3. "Life is complex.
4. "Therefore, life also has an intelligent designer."

Rejecting Paley's conclusion, Collins offers "the following parallel [counter] argument" to show the logical fallacy of Paley's argument:

1. "Electric current in my house consists of a flow of electrons.
2. "Electric current comes from the power company.
3. "Lightning consists of a flow of electrons.
4. "Therefore, lightning comes from the power company."[5]

It's an awkward comparison—even a tad silly. Paley did not set up the fake syllogism; Collins did. And it shows how far many scientists would go—even faith-friendly ones such as Collins—to discredit the most commonsense statements of faith.

Collins takes a similar tack with the position of intelligent design proponent Michael Behe. Arguing against Darwin's theory of natural selection, Behe puts forward the notion of "irreducible complexity," contending, as Collins accurately summarizes it, that intricate organic entities, such as the cells of living organisms, "could never have arisen on the basis of natural selection." And that's because "complex structures that involve the interaction of multiple proteins" could not function "if any one of those proteins is inactivated."[6] Hence, the need for an intelligent designer.

But Collins regards such reasoning as based on ignorance. Using the human eye as a case in point, he suggests that "it is not prohibitively difficult, given hundreds of millions of years, to contemplate how this system could have evolved into the modern mammalian eye, complete with light-sensing retina and light-focusing lens."[7] Thus, he dismisses Behe's commonsense position.

At the same time, however, some of the most outlandish "scientific" assertions get a pass from Collins. Physicists agree, he says, "that the universe began as an infinitely dense, dimensionless point of pure energy," followed by "the Big Bang"—14 billion years ago.[8] Collins then goes on to say that so far "scientists have been unable to interpret the very earliest events in the explosion, occupying the first 10^{-43} seconds (one tenth of a millionth of a millionth of a millionth of a millionth of a millionth of a millionth of a millionth of a second!)."[9] The statement boggles the mind, and in an odd way reveals the high degree of scientific hubris we're dealing with here—to even contemplate the possibility of discovering such a thing 14 billion years after the fact!

To give another example, Collins reports (with a straight face) that notable scientists, including the famous Francis Crick, believe that "life forms must have arrived on Earth from outer space, either carried by small particles floating through interstellar space and captured by Earth's gravity or even brought here intentionally (or accidentally) by some ancient space traveler."[10]

I have a sense that scientists can get away with such fanciful inferences because they practically control the entire field of ideas in this area without any significant opposition. By contrast, a high-drama murder trial, for example, pits powerful forces against each other, each side armed with the latest in contemporary forensic science. The apparently watertight evidence presented by one side in the morning could be upended by the other side in the afternoon. That's because competent experts are operating on both sides of the issue, with lengthy prison terms—not to mention life and death—at stake. With regard to the claims of evolutionary science, however, the "prosecution" monopolizes the "court," with little or no pushback from a beaten-down—often nonexistent—"defense."

The uncontested unanimity in the scientific community on the question of origin should strike the ordinary person as odd. After all, there's conflict and debate in just about every other area of human experience or enterprise. Over the question about what causes autism, for example—to pull things at random out of a hat; or whether one or another drug should be recalled, with reputable scientists and physicians taking up position on both sides—or whether foreign aid brings any long-term relief from poverty, disease, and conflict for those receiving it; or the benefits of so-called medical marijuana; or over what causes global warming—indeed, whether it exists at all; or over the safety (or not) of genetically modified foods; or whether standardized tests improve education; or whether annual mammograms should be recommended or not. And the list goes on, with new disputed issues arising every day.

So how is it that on this single, complicated subject of origins there seems to be so little debate? Would it be wrong to call this scientific totalitarianism?

The fact, I think, is that most people don't care. They have no personal investment in the subject—emotionally, economically, theologically, or otherwise. The issues involved do not touch their daily lives—do not determine whether they have a job or not, or whether they can put food on their table. Scientists and other interested parties can go on forever with their arcane deliberations and pronouncements, for all they care.

Such public unconcern, notwithstanding, important issues are at stake here, issues that affect the most laid-back and unsuspecting members of society—issues of truth and fallacy. And if I may borrow the words of Alister McGrath on a slightly different subject, I would make the point that Christian scientists and theologians should seek to get the message out that "the natural sciences depend on inductive inference, which is a matter of 'weighing evidence and judging probability, not proof.' " Said McGrath:

"Competing explanations are evident in every level of the human endeavor to represent the world—from the details of quantum mechanics to . . . 'ultimate questions' of meaning. . . . Any given set of observations can be explained by a number of theories. . . . There can be no question of scientific 'proof' of ultimate questions. Either we cannot answer them or we must answer them on grounds other than the sciences."[11]

3. It's much easier to tear down the other guy's position than to construct one's own.

Collins discusses four options regarding origins: atheism and agnosticism; creationism; intelligent design; and BioLogos (his own coinage to replace "theistic evolution").

He finds atheism and agnosticism unsatisfactory, distancing himself from evolutionists such as Richard Dawkins and Daniel Dennett, who advocate that "an acceptance of evolution in biology requires an acceptance of atheism in theology."[12]

Nor does Collins have much respect for creationism. The term "Creationist," he says, "has been hijacked . . . to apply to a very specific subset of . . . believers, specifically those who insist on a literal reading of Genesis 1 and 2 to describe the creation of the universe and the formation of life on earth."[13] With something bordering on scorn, he shines a light on what he calls "Young Earth Creationism." Young Earth Creationism "interprets the six days of creation as literal twenty-four-hour days," concluding "that the earth must be less than ten thousand years old."[14] And it advocates "that all species were created by individual acts of divine creation, and that Adam and Eve were historical figures created by God from dust in the Garden of Eden, and not descended from other creatures."[15]

Such beliefs Collins considers ridiculous and unacceptable.

As for the third option, Intelligent Design (ID) (intentionally capitalized),[16] Collins holds it in equally low esteem. What irks him about the ID movement is its claim to scientific standing and its emphasis on the concept of irreducible complexity (as discussed above), in opposition to Charles Darwin's evolutionary philosophy. Collins describes the movement as "a fringe activity with little credibility within the mainstream scientific community."[17]

His own position is that of theistic evolution, which he describes as "the dominant position of serious biologists who are also serious believers."[18] He lists its basic premises as follows:

1. "The universe came into being out of nothingness, approximately 14 billion years ago.

2. "Despite massive improbabilities, the properties of the universe appear to have been precisely tuned for life.

3. "While the precise mechanism of the origin of life on earth remains unknown, once life arose, the process of evolution and natural selection permitted the development of biological diversity and complexity over very long periods of time.

4. "Once evolution got under way, no special supernatural intervention was required.

5. "Humans are part of this process, sharing a common ancestor with the great apes.

6. "But humans are also unique in ways that defy evolutionary explanation and point to our spiritual nature."[19]

Collins refers to these developments as "the elegant mechanism of evolution."[20] But one has only to notice points 3, 4, and 5—especially point 5—to see the hollowness of that claim and how much it cheapens the word "elegant." (To think, for the sake of argument, that God would arrange for the eye or the brain to take millions of years to form and develop! Why, the sloppiest builder or inventor today would consider such a process utterly nonsensical and ridiculous. And to call such a process "elegant"!) Point 6, given the implications of the items that precede it, is nothing but a vapid theological sop, with no real basis in either Scripture or science.

No one understands every detail of the Genesis creation account. But the basic contours of the story are uncomplicated once one posits an omnipotent, omniscient God. Regardless of competing interpretations, the plain reading of the story would suggest that the writer understood himself to be speaking about nonfigurative, regular days. And however compact the history, the rest of Genesis—as indeed the rest of Scripture—builds upon the Creation narrative, with characters such as Adam, Eve, Cain, Abel, Noah, Abraham, Isaac, and Jacob considered real historical figures. In Romans 5:12 Paul makes the matter-of-fact statement that "sin entered the world through one man, and death through sin." "In this way," he says, "death came to all people, because all sinned." I wonder how Collins or other theistic evolutionists would explain that passage.

So what we have in front of us here—and running through the Scriptures—is what's known in theology as *Heilsgeschichte*, salvation history. A history that moves from Genesis to Revelation, from protology to eschatology, from Fall to restoration, with a strong internal logic all its own. Remove the Genesis account, and the entire system collapses.

Exactly how God did His work of creation we will never fully understand. But we impugn His character when we contort the truly elegant revelation He's given us in order to conform it to the positions of Darwinian evolution. The notion of theistic evolution upends the biblical revelation by unrecognizably disfiguring the doctrine of creation and throwing the doctrine of the Fall into total confusion. Moreover, its effect is to make suspect the entire Old Testament account of sacred history and put key elements of the Christian faith on shaky ground—elements such as the Incarnation, the atonement, the Second Coming, the Resurrection, and the afterlife. If we think that giving in on Creation makes the rest of the biblical revelation more palatable to scientists, we are simply dreaming.

4. In almost every attempt to harmonize faith and science, faith comes out the loser.

Attempts to harmonize faith and science almost invariably follow the same pattern: characterize the Genesis account as poetry or allegory, and paint those who believe otherwise as ignorant literalists. And that's what Collins does in a variety of statements throughout his book. "The description of Adam's creation from the dust of the earth, and the subsequent creation of Eve from one of Adam's ribs," he suggests, should not be considered "literal history." Rather, it is "a symbolic allegory of the entrance of the human soul into a previously soulless animal kingdom."[21] For Collins, the Genesis account of creation "can best be understood as poetry and allegory rather than a literal scientific description of origins."[22]

Incidentally, I've often wondered about the inclusion of the word "scientific" in statements like that last quote from Collins. If I see a vehicle being put together on an assembly line and I proceed to tell someone else about it, why should my account be considered as either scientific or unscientific? And if in the telling of that account, I use figures of speech—or even a touch of poetry—why should that destroy the basic factuality of my report? When the writer of Psalm 78 (see verses 9-72) recalls the Exodus and subsequent events in Israelite history in the form of poetry, how does that damage the factuality of the story?

Notwithstanding Collins' bridge-building intentions, evolution comes out the winner just about every time—as, for example, in each of the following observations: "No serious biologist today doubts the theory of evolution to explain the marvelous complexity and diversity of life"[23] "By any reasonable standard, Young Earth Creationism has reached a point of intellectual bankruptcy, both in its science and in its theology."[24] "Evolution, as a mechanism, can be and must be true."[25] "From a biologist's perspective, the evidence in favor of evolution is utterly compelling."[26]

In the face of such categorical affirmations from a heavyweight like Collins, where is the scientist with lesser credentials who would dare speak out in opposition? Collins himself inadvertently explained the psychology at work in situations of this kind. Speaking about his own choice, theistic evolution, he notes that "while many scientists ascribe to [it], they are in general reluctant to speak out for fear of negative reaction from their scientific peers."[27]

It's a revealing comment. No one, scientists included, enjoys the prospect of intellectual harassment and exclusion, which perhaps explains the deafening silence in the public arena from scientists that may entertain contrarian interpretations of the evidence before them.

Conclusion

To say that the book of Genesis does not deal with science is to state the obvious. The question, rather, is whether it deals with *fact*. And I think it does. To imply, however, that the Genesis story involves the universe, as Collins does numerous times throughout his book, is a common mistake—and a serious one. The concern of Genesis is with the earth and its immediate environs, not the universe as a whole. And the fundamental issue, as I understand it, is *the origin of life* on earth. In this regard, there is no claim of evolution that would not be open to contrarian interpretations—*if the "prosecutors" did not effectively control the "court," with the "defense" cowered into silence.*

Carefully considered, theistic evolution is fundamentally incompatible with the biblical revelation. And what at first seemed like a brilliant coup, calculated to capture the embrace of a sophisticated scientific community, turns out to be a strategic retreat, lacking in authentic biblical spine.

The Christian should have nothing but respect for science when it operates within its own sphere. Physicists and biologists, in particular, are dealing with exceedingly complicated stuff, and laypeople such as I should not even pretend to go there. But as human beings, we all have the responsibility to think and reason for ourselves. And regardless of the brilliance of the authorities in any field, we must each keep our common sense intact, and make up our own mind, in the integrity of our own conscience.

---

[1] Francis Collins, *The Language of God: A Scientist Presents Evidence for Belief* (New York: Free Press, 2006).

[2] *Ibid.*, p. 3.

[3] *Ibid.*

[4] R. Dawkins, *The God Delusion,* p. 189.

[5] Collins, pp. 86-88.

[6] *Ibid.*, p. 185, 186.

[7] *Ibid.*, p. 191.

[8] *Ibid.*, p. 65.

[9] *Ibid.*

[10] *Ibid.*, p. 91.

[11] A. E. and J. C. McGrath, *The Dawkins Delusion?* p. 35.

[12] Collins, p. 161.

[13] *Ibid.*, p. 172.

[14] *Ibid.*

[15] *Ibid.*

[16] As distinct from intelligent design in the ordinary sense—something to which Collins would subscribe.

[17] *Ibid.*, p. 187.

[18] *Ibid.*, pp. 198, 199. Collins prefers the term "Bio-Logos" (his own coinage) to the expression "theistic evolution." Bio-Logos is formed from the Greek terms *bios* (life) and *logos* (word), thus conveying the idea of life through (God's) word (p. 203).

[19] *Ibid.*, p. 200.

[20] *Ibid.*, p. 201.

[21] *Ibid.*, pp. 206, 207.

[22] *Ibid.*, p. 206.

[23] *Ibid.*, p. 99.

[24] *Ibid.*, p. 177.

[25] *Ibid.*, p. 107.

[26] *Ibid.*, p. 146.

[27] *Ibid.*, p. 202.

Chapter 4

The Motivation of God's Grace: The Force That Makes God's Mercy Tick

What's the motive behind God's scandalous grace? What's the driving force behind His mercy? Why has He been so kind to us?

Our son Dwayne was in charge of family worship at our home one evening, and an illustration he used fascinated me. It came from an article in the April 1997 issue of *National Geographic,* documenting some of the findings of the giant Hubble telescope, launched into space back in 1990.

One of the graphics in the *National Geographic* report depicted what astronomers call the Eagle Nebula. (If you have access to the Internet, why not Google it and take a look?) Named for its shape, it consists of a series of pillar-like formations, composed (according to the report) of dense, cool gas and dust.

If you did stop to take an Internet peek at this nebula, what would you guess the height of the tallest of these pillars to be? Suppose I say it's 18 million miles; that would be a fairly decent guess, wouldn't you think? But I'd be wrong—it's more than that. Suppose I erase "million" and make it 18 *billion* miles? "That'll be too much," I can hear someone say. But we'd both be wrong. According to the *National Geographic* article, the tallest of these pillars measures three light-years in height, or a distance of nearly 18 trillion miles.

And at this point my head begins to spin.

"Imagine," Dwayne said, "a spacecraft traveling at 20 miles per second, which, I understand, is the approximate speed of these machines. In one hour that craft will have traveled 72,000 miles. At that rate it would take the craft more than 28,000 years to do the distance from the bottom to the top of the tallest pillar in the nebula."

Put another way, imagine that this craft began its journey from bottom to top the day Adam was created (and I leave you to insert your own figure as to how long ago you think that was—my own assumption is in the illustration). Traveling at the fantastic speed of 72,000 miles every hour—all through the lifetime of Methuselah; through the time of Abraham; through the 400 years or so of Egyptian captivity; through the time of the judges, the kings, the prophets; through the time of Jesus and the early church; through the Middle Ages, the Reformation, the Great Disappointment, World Wars I and II; right down to this minute that you're reading this chapter—that craft will have done less than one third the distance.

And remember, we're talking about just one tiny segment of the universe! *National Geographic*, describing a camera shot to which it gave the intriguing caption "Worlds Without End," explained that Hubble pointed its lens at one of the apparently emptiest parts of the sky; focusing on a region the size of a grain of sand held at arm's length. And what it found was layer upon layer upon layer of galaxies, as far as Hubble's eyes could see![1]

You think about it for a second, and the mind shuts down in sheer astonishment and wonder. Measured on the scale of the rest of the universe, our planet (in a manner of speaking) does not exist. I laugh to myself every time I hear reports that scientists are trying to discover whether there is intelligent life elsewhere in the universe, and I think, *How mindless can we be? To even entertain the notion for a split second that in this entire colossal cosmos, intelligent life would be found only on this speck of an outpost! Sheer madness!*

No, you and I know from the inspired writings that there are literally billions and billions and billions of other beings that God has created, scattered throughout the unending vastness of space.

Yet God in Jesus Christ literally emptied heaven for us. And the question is Why? What motivated such awesome grace? What made Him do it? The answer is simple and uncomplicated. And it comes from the most well-known of all biblical passages, the mother of all soteriological pronouncements, the Magna Carta of our salvation: "For God so loved the world, that he gave his only begotten Son, that whosoever believeth in him should not perish, but have everlasting life" (John 3:16, KJV).

As regards the motivation of God's grace, what this passage says is that the impetus, the stimulus, the catalyst for that grace is *love—pure, unadulterated, unconditional love.*[2]

A (Faint) Human Example

When I think of unconditional love, the motivation behind God's grace, my mind goes back to one of the most gripping stories in the Old Testament: the story of Absalom. The narrative documents the tense, rocky relationship between the young man and his royal father, David (a tension provoked by Absalom's murder of his own half brother Amnon for sexually violating Absalom's sister Tamar). It's a long story that takes us through Absalom's self-imposed exile; his return following an ingenuous scheme devised by Joab; his temporary reconciliation with his father; and his eventual rebellion (2 Sam. 13-18).

The Bible describes the young prince as an exceedingly handsome specimen of humanity. It says in 2 Samuel 14:25 that "in all Israel there was not a man so highly praised for his handsome appearance as Absalom." "From the top of his head," says the next verse, "to the sole of his foot there was no blemish in him." When he cut his hair, the Bible says, it weighed 200 shekels (something like five pounds).

But in time that handsome head managed to hatch the deepest treason, and there came the day when a messenger rushed into the throne room of the king with the disturbing news that the king's own son had launched a coup d'état.

The account describes how the king, upon receiving the news, hastily abandons the palace and the capital, accompanied by the rest of the royal household as well as his personal bodyguards and fighting men. And David, it says, sadly, "continued up the Mount of Olives, weeping as he went; his head was covered and he was barefoot. All the people with him covered their heads too and were weeping as they went up" (2 Sam. 15:30). The picture of a broken father, crushed, devastated. The one hunting him down this time was not his envious predecessor, but his own child.

Yet as David's men prepared to engage the forces of Absalom, something exceedingly tender transpires, something that has all the smell of grace. Standing beside the gate as the troops marched out, David, in the hearing of the whole army, gives a strange command to the leaders of his forces: "Be gentle with the young man Absalom for my sake" (2 Sam. 18:5).

What incredible love!

The decisive moment of that bloody day in the forest of Ephraim is graphically described for us in verse 9: "Now Absalom happened to meet David's men. He was riding his mule, and as the mule went under the thick branches of a large oak, Absalom's hair got caught in the tree. He was left hanging in midair, while the mule he was riding kept on going."

Poetic justice, one might say. Here's this rebel caught up in a tree by his head—the same award-winning head that had plotted the bloody rebellion, resulting that day in 20,000 casualties (verse 7). Here was that head now caught in the tree, still full of murderous mischief but without any power to carry it out.

No sooner had word of the fortuitous accident come to Joab's ears than he hastened to the critical spot. Taking three javelins in his hand, he "plunged them into Absalom's heart while Absalom was still alive in the oak tree. And ten of Joab's armor-bearers surrounded" the young prince and finished him off (verses 14, 15).

The most poignant part of the story comes right here—after the king learns that Absalom is dead. "The king was shaken," the narrative says. "He went up to the room over the gateway and wept. As he went, he said: 'O my son Absalom! My son, my son, Absalom! If only I had died instead of you—O Absalom, my son, my son!'" (verse 33).

The Perfect Manifestation

Two thousand years ago the One whom many of His contemporaries called "Jesus, son of David" traversed the same grounds as did his ancient human father. And from the Mount of Olives, days before His death, as He looked down upon a city full of Absaloms, His heart, like David's, broke: "O Jerusalem, Jerusalem," I paraphrase Him, "if only you knew! If only you knew!" (See Matt. 23:37; Luke 19:41-44.)

Today we know that it wasn't Roman blows and nails that killed Him. It was *we* who murdered Him. And yet He loves us still!

In Jesus we see the embodiment of unconditional love—which is not as easy a concept to get one's head around as many mistakenly think. In Fyodor Dostoyevsky's *The Brothers Karamazov* the agnostic Ivan (one of the Karamazov brothers) poses difficult situations to confound his religious-leaning sibling. He tells the story of atrocities committed by soldiers of a certain country there in Central Europe, soldiers who "burned villages, murdered, [and] outraged women and children." "[They] took a pleasure in torturing children . . . tossing babies up in the air and catching them on the points of their bayonets before their mothers' eyes."

Then Ivan proceeded to what he considered the ultimate atrocity: "Imagine a trembling mother with her baby in her arms, a circle of invading [soldiers] around her. They've planned a diversion: they pet the baby, laugh to make it laugh. They succeed, the baby laughs. At that moment a [soldier] points a pistol four inches from the baby's face. The baby laughs with glee, holds out its little hands to the pistol, and [at that very instant the soldier] pulls the trigger in the baby's face and blows out its brains."[3]

Who among us has arrived at the place where we find it easy to love such beasts in human skin?

But what my Bible tells me, and the point of that great "whosoever" in John 3:16, is that there is Somebody in the universe who actually loves the vilest, the wickedest, and the most contemptible human being on the face of the planet, and who would give His life all over again for them alone. Some of you reading this may understand such love. I confess I cannot begin to fathom it.

But that's what motivated God's grace—sheer, unadulterated, unconditional love. Love that reaches out to you and me, no matter who we are, where we are, or what we are. However degraded we might be or feel, the Hound of Heaven is on our trail and will never give up the chase until there's utterly no hope left. God looks past the externals and sees some spark that He can nurture into life, some little flame He can rekindle.

> "Down in the human heart,
> Crushed by the tempter,
> Feelings lie buried that grace can restore."[4]

I can fall in love with a Savior like that, can't you? Over the centuries many have. And the grace of God looks forward to that grand moment when millions and millions from this minuscule outpost of the universe will gather 'round the Savior in the kingdom, saved by His blood.

What astonishing love is this!

---

[1] The site indicated by the URL below probably has its own agenda, but it was the only one I was able to find quickly, carrying the particular image referred to in the *National Geographic* article: http://www.greaterthings.com/Topical/Multiple_Mortalities/soul_born.htm. For the sake of those who might have taken a look at the link, I might observe that according to the *National Geographic* report only a few objects in the picture are individual stars, which appear as spiked points of light. Everything else is a galaxy, each one containing billions of stars. And the closest of these galaxies to us is 4 billion light-years! (I also found quite engaging this five-minute YouTube clip entitled "Our Awesome Universe—Galaxies Without End": http://www.youtube.com/watch?v=_rnNRKHKIyI.)

[2] Please note that I'm talking here about *unconditional love,* not *unconditional acceptance.* In my thinking, it's dangerous to confuse the two.

[3] Fyodor Dostoyevsky, *The Brothers Karamazov* (New York: Bantam Dell, 1970), part 2, book 5, chap. 4.

[4] Fannie J. Crosby, "Rescue the Perishing."

Chapter 5

How God Saves the Nations: Understanding This Will Reset Our Concept of His Love

A Seventh-day Adventist brother once let me in on a debate between him and his wife. It arose from a statement in an article I'd written on Japan in the August 14, 2003, issue of *Adventist Review*. My reference to an Adventist membership in Japan (at the time) of just under 15,000 in a population of 126.5 million had led him to the conclusion that "Christ is not about to return, because millions of people in Japan have not [yet] heard the gospel." But his wife argued to the contrary "that every person in Japan has heard the good news . . . but they have [not] accepted it."

The disagreement notwithstanding, their basic presuppositions were the same—namely, that the gospel must go to every person on earth before Jesus can come. The only difference was that the wife believed (in the case of Japan) that it had, while the husband believed it had not. Both positions are important in their own right, but it's the wife's position that's at once more problematic and more intriguing. What was her basis for saying that the population of Japan had heard the gospel? And how did she come to the conclusion they'd rejected it?

To whatever extent, the concern of this couple is the concern of most Adventists. We look at the great mass of humanity in the non-Christian regions of the world, and we wonder how the gospel can possibly reach them in any meaningful way any time soon. Millions, moreover, are dying every day, and millions more are being born.

Faced with this statistical nightmare, yet wanting to preserve our belief in an imminent Advent, some among us (such as the wife in our story) argue either that those billions have, indeed, heard and rejected God's offer of grace or that there'd be untold millions in the kingdom who will never have heard the name of Jesus or been exposed to the gospel. "The salvation of a man on the other side of the world," argued one of our scholars in a research paper years ago, does not depend "on the actions of a man on this side." Adventists are coming to realize, he said, "that as a church we are in the stream of history. . . . The human race is one." And just as we can admit "that a Methodist might be saved without being an Adventist," so we should be prepared to "admit that a Confucianist might be saved without becoming a Christian."[1]

How do we sort this all out?

In what follows, I briefly explore the shift in thinking that occurred during the first part of the nineteenth century among some mainline Protestant churches in the United States regarding the historic Christian belief of salvation in Jesus alone. Next, I list (with only minimum comment) the three New Testament passages that feature most prominently in the issue before us. And finally, I give a brief overview of statements from the writings of Ellen G. White as they relate to the New Testament passages in question and the issue of the salvation of the nations.

Envisioning Salvation Apart From Christ

The early nineteenth century witnessed a huge drive in Christian mission. One of the greatest since Pentecost, it was fanned by the belief that personal faith in Christ was absolutely necessary for salvation. That there might be saving light from any other source was unthinkable. But 100 years later doubts began to emerge. A century of Christian mission having manifestly failed to break through the bulwarks of the entrenched non-Christian establishment in the world, voices began calling for a reappraisal of the church's foreign mission strategy.

Pursuant to this concern a group of lay Christians met in New York in 1930 and drew up proposals that eventually led to the formation of the (interdenominational) Laymen's Foreign Missions Inquiry (LFMI) in order to reevaluate the nature and purpose of mission.[2]

That reevaluation, carried out by the Institute of Social and Religious Research (working under the auspices of the LFMI), focused in particular on India, Burma, China, and Japan. At the conclusion of its work the institute handed over its findings for analysis to yet another body: the 15-member Commission of Appraisal, headed by William E. Hocking, professor of philosophy at Harvard University.

In its report, entitled *Re-thinking Missions* (1932), the commission criticized the traditional belief that pictured "millions of souls" in Asia as "in danger of eternal death . . . [with] but one way [to life], the way of Christ." The mature Christian community, the commission said, has long since outgrown such antiquated motives.[3] Without actually proposing the discontinuance of mission, the report suggested, nevertheless, that missionaries should consider themselves coworkers with the leaders of non-Christian religions, not competitors.[4] "The final truth, whatever it may be," the report said, "is the New Testament of every existing faith."[5] Mature Christians should abandon the concept of hell and punishment for "happier concepts of destiny."[6]

Several years later, in 1939, Hocking spelled out what his commission had veiled in more careful language: "Today, through the penetrating power of commerce and science, something like a world culture begins to appear. With it, the question is bound to arise whether a world religion is not a necessary accompaniment of world culture." Hocking believed it was. In the "sharp light" of a world religion, he said, "all one's localisms are seen to be local, and therefore unessential, relative, queer, afflicted with the staleness of ancient subjectivities, like a stuffy air which one can no longer endure to breathe once one has been outside in the freshness of a great morning." Then came his startling conclusion: "God is in his world, but Buddha, Jesus, Muhammad are in their little private closets, and we shall thank them, but never return to them. Such is the spirit of world citizenship at the moment."[7]

How the Scriptures See It

At least three passages in the New Testament speak more or less directly to the issue before us: John 1:9, Romans 1:20, and Romans 2:12-15. Each provides its own answers but also leads to other important questions.

John 1:9: "That was the true Light which gives light to every man coming into the world" (NKJV).

In the incisive words of Rubin Widmer, we may ask the following questions:

"What is the true light? How is every man lighted? Does this phrase mean that every man born into the world is given through conscience, or some other avenue, sufficient light for his salvation? Does 'every man' mean literally every single individual born into the world, or does it mean that every man who receives spiritual light receives it from Christ as the source? Does the light of salvation come to every man in the world independent of the preaching of the gospel? Can men in so-called heathen lands be saved without ever coming in contact with the gospel message? Does redemptive knowledge come only through the gospel? If men do not receive salvation apart from the gospel, then do those who never hear the gospel story have a chance to be saved? In other words, are they lost because they failed to follow whatever 'light' they had, or are they lost because the gospel light never reached them?"[8]

These are tough questions, but they are absolutely critical.

Romans 1:20: "For since the creation of the world God's invisible qualities—his eternal power and divine nature—have been clearly seen, being understood from what has been made, so that people are without excuse."

The questions here, says Widmer, are the following: "What are the invisible things which may be 'clearly seen'? Who can clearly see these in nature?" Can "everyone who comes in contact with the natural world . . . understand enough in nature to choose eternal salvation—or reject it? . . . Whatever this is that can be seen in nature, is it sufficient for salvation?"[9]

Romans 2:12-15: "All who sin apart from the law will also perish apart from the law, and all who sin under the law will be judged by the law. . . . (Indeed, when Gentiles, who do not have the law, do by nature things required by the law, they are a law for themselves. . . . They show that the requirements of the law are written on their hearts, their consciences also bearing witness, and their thoughts sometimes accusing them and at other times even defending them.)"

"Does [Paul] teach," asks Widmer, "that Gentiles have by nature an inner law of conscience which, if they follow, will save them without any knowledge of the gospel? Is salvation then based on righteousness by works apart from faith in Christ?"[10]

Widmer has done a commendable job raising the right questions, and his answers are important. But biblical scholars and missiologists have batted these issues around forever. And rather than simply add to the debate with ideas of my own, I want instead to take a look at the contribution to the discussion of one of the nineteenth century's most insightful religious writers, Ellen G. White. Without engaging the problem head-on, she has made comments that get at the heart of the issue.

What She Said

Over the years I've run into many Adventists who, whether out of careless speech or studied conviction, believe that millions of people will be saved apart from a knowledge or acceptance of Jesus or the gospel. And most of those who espouse this position think they are supported by the three New Testament passages mentioned above and by the writings of Ellen G. White.

So what exactly did Ellen White say?

Speaking of the method employed by Paul and his companions in their preaching, Ellen White says, instructively, that they avoided "complicated, far-fetched reasoning," dwelling instead on "the attributes of the Creator of the world, the Supreme Ruler of the universe. Their hearts aglow with the love of God and of His Son," she says, "they appealed to the heathen to behold the infinite sacrifice made in man's behalf. They knew that if those who had long been groping in the darkness of heathenism could but see the light streaming from Calvary's cross, they would be drawn to the Redeemer."[11]

Three elements stand out in this description of the apostle's witnessing strategy: God as Creator, Jesus as Savior, and a call for acceptance. What Paul and his companions presented to those outside the pale of Judaism, she seemed to be saying, constituted the essential bedrock of the gospel.

Ellen White, citing Scripture, speaks of Jesus as "the name that is above every name, the only name given among men whereby men can be saved."[12] "God is approached," she says, "through Jesus Christ, the Mediator. . . . This is the sinner's only hope. . . . There is only one channel."[13]

We may deduce from the above that the doctrine that constitutes the sine qua non (the absolute essential) for salvation for every cognitive person on earth is the doctrine of the atonement, however rudimentary the form it takes—the simple personal knowledge and acceptance of Jesus Christ and His atoning sacrifice in our behalf.

So, then, did Ellen White believe the nations are lost if we don't reach them?

The church's indolence was a matter of great concern for Ellen White. For her, Christian responsibility is fact, not fiction. "Many have gone down to ruin," she says, "who might have been saved if their neighbors, common men and women, had put forth personal effort for them."[14] "Multitudes perish for want of Christian teaching. Beside our own doors and in foreign lands the heathen are untaught and unsaved."[15]

Getting It Right

In a matter fraught with such grave consequence for the destiny of large sectors of humanity, it's critical that we get it right. We are terribly misguided if we do not see a vast difference between a Methodist and a Confucianist.

Nevertheless, the question is If Christians prove indolent, neglecting their duty in spreading the gospel, is all lost?

Ellen White's answer would be no—all is not lost.

But we ought to notice carefully how she puts the case: "As through Christ every human being has life," she wrote, "so also through Him every soul receives some ray of divine light. Not only intellectual but spiritual power, a perception of right, a desire for goodness, exists in every heart."[16]

But was it her position that that light can save in and of itself?

Though not a trained theologian, Ellen White makes her way through these theological explosives with consummate insight and skill. "Among all nations, kindreds, and tongues," she says, the Lord "sees men and women who are praying for light and knowledge. Their souls are unsatisfied; long have they fed on ashes. . . . But they are honest in heart and desire to learn a better way. Although in the depths of heathenism, with no knowledge of the written law of God nor of His Son Jesus, they have revealed in manifold ways the working of a divine power on mind and character."[17]

However, this honesty of heart is not salvation. This longing for something better is not itself that something. And so it is a matter of critical significance to note what follows the above remarks: "this Light [that the "heathen" individual has received]," she continues, "if heeded, will guide his feet to the kingdom of God."[18] Therefore, even this light requires a response in order to be effectual in the individual's life—as is true for everyone else.

What we need is a more careful reading of Ellen White—as in the following, for example: "In the depths of heathenism, men who have had no knowledge of the written law of God, who have never even heard the name of Christ, have been kind to His servants, protecting them at the risk of their own lives. Their acts show the working of a divine power."[19]

We might note that up to this point in the statement, Ellen White says nothing about salvation. Only later does she come to that. And when she does, her theology is as careful as ever (though you may want to pardon her politically incorrect language—she wrote at a different time, obviously): "Their acts show the working of a divine power. The Holy Spirit has implanted the grace of Christ in the heart of the savage, quickening his sympathies contrary to his nature, contrary to his education. The 'Light which lighteth every man that cometh into the world' . . . is shining in his soul; and this light, if heeded, will guide his feet to the kingdom of God."[20]

Now, Watch This!

Someone may ask at this point, "Does not Ellen White say that many people will be saved who have never seen or heard the human messenger?" The answer to this question is yes, and that should bring immense reassurance to all who love the people of the world. I come to this point only now so as not in any way to detract from the importance of Christian responsibility.

The human messenger represents what might be called God's modus operandi, God's chosen method of operation. But if through indolence no human agent reaches a poor soul struggling for light in a deprived area of the world, God in His infinite mercy has in reserve, so to speak, an ultima ratio—a last resort, a special arrangement to bypass an otherwise fatal obstacle.

At least two statements from Ellen White bring this out, each throwing light on the other. The matter is extremely delicate, and we should read these statements with utmost care: "Among the heathen are those who worship God ignorantly, those to whom the light is never brought by human instrumentality, yet they will not perish. Though ignorant of the written law of God, they have heard His voice speaking to them in nature, and have done the things that the law required. Their works are evidence that the Holy Spirit has touched their hearts, and they are recognized as the children of God."[21]

Here she clearly states that the light has not been brought by "human instrumentality." But she does not say that the light has not been brought at all! In fact, apart from attributing it to the operation of the Holy Spirit, she gives, in the second statement, another clue as to how the light would come to this special class: "The angels of heaven are sent forth to minister to those who shall be heirs of salvation. We know not now who they are . . . but angels of heaven are passing throughout the length and breadth of the earth, seeking to . . . win the hearts of men to Christ. Not one is neglected or passed by. God is no respecter of persons, and He has an equal care for all the souls He has created."[22]

What a beautiful description of the character of a loving God!

So in regard to the spousal debate on the progress of the gospel in Japan mentioned at the beginning, we would have to say, in the light of all the evidence, that as human beings we do not know, nor can we know, the status of the situation as God Himself sees it—in Japan or anywhere else. Considering all the relevant factors, however, the safe approach—for us and for those in darkness—is that we work as if we were the only agents at God's disposal.

Only after we've done all we can must we allow ourselves to dwell on the fact—and it is a fact—that when all else fails, God, in His inscrutable wisdom and grace, has in reserve an ultima ratio—a last resort, a special arrangement to bypass an otherwise fatal obstacle to the salvation of the nations, namely, the deployment of supernatural agencies to the rescue.

Feast your heart, then, on this final word that sums up all the rest, and notice how skillfully Ellen White brings out the essentials of salvation:

"Heaven's plan of salvation is broad enough to embrace the whole world. God longs to breathe into prostrate humanity the breath of life. And He will not permit any soul to be disappointed who is sincere in his longing for something higher and nobler than anything the world can offer. Constantly He is sending His angels to those who, while surrounded by circumstances the most discouraging, pray in faith for some power higher than themselves to take possession of them and bring deliverance and peace. In various ways God will reveal Himself to them and will place them in touch with providences that will establish their confidence in the One who has given Himself a ransom for all."[23]

What a God!

---

[1] G. H. Minchin, "The Salvation of the Heathen" (unpublished paper, Ellen G. White Research Center, Andrews University), p. 7.

[2] Members of the inquiry came from seven denominations: (Northern) Baptist, Congregational, Methodist, Episcopal, Presbyterian Church in the United States, Reformed Church in America, and United Presbyterian.

[3] William E. Hocking (chair, Commission of Appraisal), *Re-thinking Missions: A Laymen's Inquiry After One Hundred Years* (New York: Harper and Brothers, 1932), p. 8.

[4] *Ibid.*, p. 40

[5] *Ibid.*, p. 44.

[6] *Ibid.*, p. 19.

[7] William E. Hocking, *Living Religions and a World Faith* (London: G. Allen & Unwin Ltd., 1940), pp. 21, 22.

[8] Rubin Widmer, *Jesus, the Light of the World* (Nashville: Southern Pub. Assn., 1967), pp. 9, 10.

[9] *Ibid.*, p. 11.

[10] *Ibid.*

[11] Ellen G. White, *The Acts of the Apostles* (Mountain View, Calif.: Pacific Press Pub. Assn., 1911), pp. 248, 249.

[12] Ellen G. White, *Selected Messages* (Washington, D.C.: Review and Herald Pub. Assn., 1958, 1980), book 1, p. 333; see also Ellen G. White, *The Ministry of Healing* (Mountain View, Calif.: Pacific Press Pub. Assn., 1905), p. 179.

[13] *The Seventh-day Adventist Bible Commentary,* Ellen G. White Comments (Washington, D.C.: Review and Herald Pub. Assn., 1953-1957), vol. 7, pp. 912, 913.

[14] Ellen G. White, *The Desire of Ages* (Mountain View, Calif.: Pacific Press Pub. Assn., 1898), p. 141.

[15] E. G. White, *The Ministry of Healing,* p. 288.

[16] Ellen G. White, *Education* (Mountain View, Calif.: Pacific Press Pub. Assn., 1903), p. 29.

[17] Ellen G. White, *Prophets and Kings* (Mountain View, Calif.: Pacific Press Pub. Assn., 1917), p. 376.

[18] *Ibid.*, p. 377. (Italics supplied.) Ellen G. White, *Christ's Object Lessons* (Washington, D.C.: Review and Herald Pub. Assn., 1900), p. 385.

[19] E. G. White, *Christ's Object Lessons,* p. 385.

[20] *Ibid.* (Italics supplied.)

[21] E. G. White, *The Desire of Ages,* p. 638.

[22] *Ibid.*, p. 639.

[23] E. G. White, *Prophets and Kings,* pp. 377, 378.

Chapter 6

Every Thought Captive: The Toughest Battle We're Called to Fight

For though we live in the world, we do not wage war as the world does. The weapons we fight with are not the weapons of the world. On the contrary, they have divine power to demolish strongholds. We demolish arguments and every pretension that sets itself up against the knowledge of God, and we take captive every thought to make it obedient to Christ" (2 Cor. 10:3-5).[1]

I see three main elements in this passage: the weapons; the target; and the outcome.

The Weapons

The nations of antiquity (e.g., the Assyrians, Babylonians, Persians, Mongols, and Greeks) had one major craving in common: a thirst for conquest and power. Each took a map of the world they knew, decided which areas they wanted to conquer, then dispatched their armies to do the job. Alexander the Great, from whose (former) territory Paul was writing the book of 2 Corinthians, had extended his empire from the Adriatic Sea all the way to the Indus River—a huge chunk of real estate.

But as Paul was writing his letter, it was the Romans who were in charge. Roman influence and power covered the entire region, extending by force the mandates of the Caesars. As he journeyed from Ephesus to Macedonia, from where he'd write the words that concern us here, Paul would have encountered multiple outposts of heavily armed Roman soldiers, providing a sharp contrast between the strategy of worldly conquest and the message of the cross. Thus the choice of words at the beginning of the passage: "For though we live in the world, we do not wage war as the world does. The weapons we fight with are not the weapons of the world."

Across the centuries the Christian church has faced the continuing temptation to de-emphasize (if not abandon altogether) this spiritual, nonviolent strategy in favor of worldly methodologies and approaches. The classic example of this came during medieval times, when tens of thousands of European Christians took up arms and, in a number of separate missions, went out to the Holy Land shedding blood in Jesus' name. The Crusades stand out as one of the darkest chapters in the history of Christianity.

But the New Testament is all about nonviolence when it comes to the message and mission of the gospel. "Put that sword back," Jesus said to Peter during a tense confrontation in the Garden of Gethsemane the night of His arrest (Matt. 26:52, my paraphrase). And standing before Pilate the next day, He said: "My kingdom is not of this world. If it were, my servants would fight to prevent my arrest" (John 18:36).

So if "the sword" is not our weapon, what is it?

Paul does not define this detail in the passage before us. But after encountering "beasts" at Ephesus (1 Cor. 15:32), he listed at least two of the armaments we need to face the deadly contingent from the underworld: "the sword of the Spirit, which is the word of God," and prayer (Eph. 6:17, 18).

Corinth was a sophisticated, immoral city—Paris, New York, and Bangkok rolled into one. And Paul's remarks were directed to believers fresh from that heady, urban milieu, facing the temptation to employ worldly methods and approaches to advance the gospel.

We face a similar temptation today. A while back I came across a magazine article about the influence games played out in Washington, D.C., perhaps the most power-driven capital in the world. I was reading about influence games surrounding food, of all things. "In the nation's capital," the article says, "power-seekers follow the powerful, especially when it comes to dining"—to places such as the Occidental Grill, the Bombay Club, the Oval Room, West 24, the Caucus Room, and Jeffrey's at the Watergate. At the Caucus Room, the article continues, "the martini glass could double as an umbrella," the wine goblet could "serve equally well as a decanter," and the whiskey tumbler, "poured tall, feels like a barrel in the hand." Patrons "sit back, relax, . . . scanning the crowd [and] wondering whom they will see and by whom they will be seen."

"Lobbyists, White House aides, lawmakers, Cabinet functionaries, news reporters," the bigwigs and top dogs of the nation and of the world—they all head to such places—each relying "on the power breakfast, [the power] lunch, [the power] dinner to get their jobs done."[2]

That's how the world wields power. That's how the world understands power. That's how the movers and shakers of the planet play the game. But Paul says, "Though we live in the world, we do not wage war as the world does." We cannot ape the methods of the world and expect lasting results for the kingdom of God. Our chief "weapons" must be the Word of God and prayer.

The Target

We do not wage war as the world does because our target is utterly different. Adventists, of all Christians, understand that we're in the midst of a vicious, titanic struggle—"not against flesh and blood," but against what Paul describes as "the powers of this dark world" and "the spiritual forces of evil in the heavenly realms" (Eph. 6:12). And these "spiritual forces," as real as you and I, have their hands in all the big crises we face today, be they intellectual, social, moral, or spiritual.

Identifying the targets against which the Christian weapon is directed, Paul refers to "arguments" and "pretensions": "We demolish arguments and every pretension that sets itself up against the knowledge of God" (2 Cor. 10:5).

The Greek word translated "arguments" is *logismos* and refers to reasoning, reflection, thought, calculation (in the cognitive sense). In this context Paul uses the word in the negative to signify ancient sophistries parading as truth but calculated to blind us to the reality of God and His claims upon our lives. "Pretension" (from the Greek word *hupsoma*—normally referring to height or exaltation) refers in the present context to human pride, to empty human pomposity that sets itself up against the sacred, to human insolence that shakes its fist in the face of God.

For Paul these "arguments" and "pretensions" stand in opposition to the "knowledge of God." They're not only anti-God but also, in a sense, rivals of God, exalting themselves against the knowledge of God. The enemy's strategy is to gum up the work of the gospel with all kinds of contrarian theories, concepts, philosophies, and ideologies so as to eclipse from the human mind and consciousness the knowledge of the true God who created the cosmos and who upholds it every hour.

In this respect one may think of the challenge posed by false science. Every Adventist Christian who enters a science classroom in a secular educational institution today faces this challenge. There's no one so intolerant as a narrow-minded liberal professor determined to foist upon their students the philosophy of a mechanistic universe devoid of God.

The Christian weapons are directed against such targets.

The Outcome

Commenting on the final outcome of this titanic struggle, Paul says: "We take captive every thought to make it obedient to Christ" (2 Cor. 10:5).

At an international conference on preaching in Cambridge, England, in April 2007 I heard world-famous New Testament scholar N. T. Wright make the point that Paul's use of pagan poets in his address on Mars' Hill (Acts 17) illustrated an attempt to take captive every thought and make it obedient to Christ. Today we should be doing the same in every field of endeavor—in religion, in the arts, in literature, in science, in industry, and in commerce. Christians are God's (not-so-secret) agents in the world, seeking to infiltrate every field of human endeavor and conscript, whenever possible, every idea and thought into the service of Christ.

There's also a personal, subjective dimension to this process of taking every thought captive—in other words, a dimension that happens inside us. We must internally "take captive every thought to make it obedient to Christ." That's huge! Have you ever tried marshaling your thoughts to bring them under control? Do you sometimes find that the more you try not to think about some things, the more you think about them—as if the very mind you're trying to control is controlling you?

The apostle is talking here about the highest level of Christian maturity. It's a tall order. And we may well ask: Who is able to accomplish this, confronted as we are with every kind of distraction and enticement literally everywhere we turn today? Who can keep their thoughts secure and inviolate?

But I keep remembering Jesus' response when in the face of a difficult statement on His part His disciples asked Him: "Who then can be saved?" (Matt. 19:25). His response: "With man this is impossible, but with God all things are possible" (verse 26). It's in God's strength alone that we're able to "take captive every thought to make it obedient to Christ."

So as I meditate on that last clause in the light of God's power, I see in my mind's eye the picture of all kinds of aberrant thoughts marching in procession as prisoners of war behind Christ the Conqueror: prideful thoughts; discouraging thoughts; immoral thoughts; lustful thoughts; thoughts of superiority over others; thoughts of inferiority to others; thoughts of secret, personal vices; thoughts of rebellion and insubordination. I see all these thoughts that molest and defeat us marching with their tails between their legs behind our cosmic Liberator, subdued and defeated by His awesome power.

We may not be there yet. But if we never think it, we'll never yearn for it. And if we never yearn for it, we'll never plead for it. And if we never plead for it, we'll never experience it.

We have a big task before us. But it's a spiritual mission, requiring divinely sanctioned "weapons." Empowered by a force beyond ourselves, we must move into a fractured, broken world with the healing power of the gospel, taking every thought—external and internal—captive to the obedience of Jesus Christ, our conquering Lord.

---

[1] For an engaging commentary on this passage, see R.C.H. Lenski, *The Interpretation of St. Paul's First and Second Epistles to the Corinthians* (Minneapolis: Augsburg Pub. House, 1963), pp. 1202-1208.

[2] Barry Lynn, "Following the Leader," *American Way*, June 1, 2001, pp. 62-69.

CHAPTER 7

When People Hurt: Deep Anger Can Result—Even at God

I could sense the pain; I could almost feel the hurt. Something bad had happened, and she was angry.

It was Sabbath afternoon, and I'd just finished speaking at a local church in Sydney, Australia. As many came forward to shake hands, to extend greetings, to chat, one couple waited silently. They needed a little more uninterrupted time with me than a brief, casual greeting.

When we finally sat down together, the wife opened up the issue they wanted to discuss. In my talk I'd dwelt at considerable length on God's love, God's mercy, God's forgiving tenderness. My emphasis had impressed her, but in a way I had not expected.

"I was abused as a child," she said as our conversation started, "in every way you can imagine."

In cases like that I never press for details—too painful for them, too embarrassing for me. But it was clear from the tone of her remarks that her father had been the culprit. And now, as is common in such cases, she found herself facing a crisis of confidence in God as a loving heavenly Father.

"Sometimes I blame God for allowing these things to happen to me," she said in suppressed anger. "I say to Him [and I could sense the deep pain in her voice], 'How could You, a loving Father, have stood there and let it happen? Could it be You just don't care?' " Strong sentiments, as she herself admitted. "One moment I blurt out words of anger," she said, "the next moment I'm scared. Is that blasphemy?" she asked me. "Is it a sin to think this way? Will God forgive me?"

Today's media being saturated with reports about all kinds of physical and sexual abuse, it's virtually impossible to be unaware of the shockingly common existence of this terrible problem. For many of us, however, our knowledge or awareness of the issue is purely theoretical. But those who've had to deal with it in counseling situations know that no press accounts can match the pressing reality of facing the anger and utter brokenness of a live person sitting in front of you. It's a nightmare that can't get much worse. You come away from a conversation like that wondering whom you can trust. And while we should not become paranoid on this point, it ought to make us less naive than we have probably been—especially in those areas of church life in which adults interact with young children. The Pathfinder Club, for example, with all its varied opportunities for physical contact; overnight trips; outings; pajama parties; etc.

But in cases like this woman's there seems so little the church or any other external entity can do. For here innocent little children are getting hurt behind closed doors *in their own homes*! And often in the end, as in this woman's case, God picks up the blame. "Could it be You just don't care?" she had said to God.

"If such emotions are genuinely in our hearts," I told her, "then God wants us to come to Him with them—however raw, however negative, however pointed. Go back and read the Psalms again," I said.

"Yes, yes!" she responded in excited agreement, as if I'd touched on something she'd always known but temporarily had forgotten.

The Psalms, indeed, have been a source of comfort to millions through the centuries largely because they're so honest. Hear the pathos in the following lines:

"O Jehovah, why have you thrown my life away? Why are you turning your face from me, and looking the other way? . . . I stand helpless before your terrors. Your fierce wrath has overwhelmed me. Your terrors have cut me off. . . . Lover, friend, acquaintance—all are gone. There is only darkness everywhere" (Ps. 88:14-18, TLB). No mincing words here; the sacred writer is confronting God head on.

Other Bible writers are equally direct. "I loathe my life," Job moaned in the midst of calamity and personal tragedy. "I will give free utterance to my complaint; I will speak in the bitterness of my soul. I will say to God, Do not condemn me; let me know why you contend against me. Does it seem good to you to oppress, to despise the work of your hands?" (Job 10:1-3, NRSV).

And Jeremiah, in the midst of his distress, did not hold back much: "You deceived me," he said to God (Jer. 20:7). Imagine the deep hurt that would wring such biting words from the lips of a reverent prophet!

And why did Jeremiah feel he'd been deceived? Undoubtedly because of the strong promises he'd been given at his call. "Today I have made you a fortified city," God had assured him, "an iron pillar and a bronze wall to stand against the whole land. . . . They will fight against you but will not overcome you, for I am with you and will rescue you" (Jer. 1:18, 19).

Now, under the sharp sting of a hurting back, blistered from severe beatings, and with the shameful public humiliation of being placed in the stocks fresh in his mind, Jeremiah descended into a state of utter brokenness and depression. "Cursed be the day I was born!" he groaned. "Cursed be the man who brought my father the news, who made him very glad, saying, 'A child is born to you—a son!' May that man be like the towns the Lord overthrew without pity. . . . For he did not kill me in the womb, with my mother as my grave. . . . Why did I ever come out of the womb to see trouble and sorrow and to end my days in shame?" (Jer. 20:14-18).

Suffering. Affliction. Pain. These words describe the human story from start to finish, our own times being right up there with the worst of them. Think of the former Yugoslavia, Rwanda, Cambodia, Angola, Northern Ireland, Syria, Zimbabwe, Congo, Sudan. The catastrophes associated with each of these countries and regions have racked up their dismal toll in suffering and human misery of every description. The hurt, the pain, the disillusionment of millions whose poignant cries for help attracted no human ear, whose unspeakable agony invited no supernatural response, no divine rescue.

Hence the biting questions—as from the lips of that hurting woman in a Sydney church that Sabbath afternoon many years ago. It's devastating to watch the long-term effect of sexual abuse on its victims. Those of us who have been spared such violations may find it difficult to grasp the enormity of such horrendous trauma. That kind of abuse scars people for life. And I think there's got to be a special judgment for adults who cause such brutal damage to the most helpless and innocent among us. Jesus was perhaps hinting at that when He said, "If any of you put a stumbling block before one of these little ones who believe in me, it would be better for you if a great millstone were fastened around your neck and you were drowned in the depth of the sea" (Matt. 18:6, NRSV).

Just imagine what He would say to the perpetrators of the hideous crime discussed here!

Jesus came to put an end to human tragedy. "He was despised and rejected by mankind," Isaiah wrote of Him, "a man of suffering, and familiar with pain" (Isa. 53:3). He is the answer to human pain. In the midst of poverty we can look to Him, for He knew what it meant to be destitute. In the midst of ridicule we can turn to Him, for He knew the sting that came from being insulted. And in the midst of tragedy we can lean on Him "because he poured out his life unto death" (verse 12). "He was oppressed and afflicted, yet he did not open his mouth; he was led like a lamb to the slaughter" (verse 7).

His suffering was not simply to console those who suffer by showing that He is a fellow sufferer—indeed, the Prince of sufferers. Rather, it was for the sake of putting an end to suffering forever. "He was wounded for our transgressions, crushed for our iniquities; upon him was the punishment that made us whole, and by his bruises we are healed" (verse 5, NRSV).

His was the suffering to end all suffering. He suffered as a human being, for He was human. But He suffered, too, as Deity, for He was God—and this we cannot fathom. The psalmist might feel forlorn; Jeremiah might feel abandoned; and that woman in a Sydney church might feel the pain of personal violation. But they suffered for themselves, each one. Nor could all their misery put together equal the anguish that wrung from the Savior's lips the heartrending cry that dark Friday outside Jerusalem: " '*Eli, Eli, lema sabachthani?*' (which means, 'My God, my God, why have you forsaken me?' ") (Matt. 27:46).

He suffered to end our pain. He died so we might live. And when all the facts are in, the whole universe, including that dear young woman who encountered me that Sabbath afternoon in a Sydney church, will shout together: "Just and true are your ways, King of the nations " (Rev. 15:3).

And there will be no more pain, no more hurt.

Chapter 8

Peace Like a River: An Experience That Eludes Too Many of Us

Oh, that you had heeded My commandments! Then your peace would have been like a river" (Isa. 48:18, NKJV).

Late in the afternoon one day during my first visit to Paris, I stood leaning over the rail of one of the many bridges spanning La Seine, that historic river flowing through the heart of this famous city. The sun was setting as a pleasure boat filled with tourists slowly floated its way down the river. On a bench along the paved riverbank far below me sat a lone couple, lazily watching the famous stream idle by. With streets in that section of the city becoming more and more deserted, I just stood there drinking in the solitude. It was a superbly peaceful feeling.

What a contrast, I thought, between that quiet moment and the violent history of France played out upon the waters below me. For that very river moving peacefully through the French metropolis on its way to the English Channel had witnessed some of the deadliest plots and political intrigues ever to flow from human breast and had stood between some of the most hostile factions ever to rise in battle.

The passions and intrigues, with their instigators and victims, have long since perished, but the peaceful river continues its flow undaunted to the sea.

Could the ancient prophet have had something like that in mind when he wrote the words of our text? I think he did.

Perhaps the deepest yearning of the human soul is the yearning for peace. So many of us are bothered by chronic problems that keep us awake nights, robbing us of precious sleep. So many of us are apprehensive about the future, concerned about what it holds for us in its mysterious hands. Some of us wake up in the night haunted by the forebodings of awful things about to happen to us.

In many industrialized societies today it has become chic to retain the permanent services of a psychiatrist. But without diminishing the need for such professionals in any way, I maintain that the implied promise of the passage before us is that those who hearken to God's commandments will experience what the prophet called "peace . . . like a river."

What Does That Mean?

However worldly or secular, we each have a conscience, an inner voice that stings us when we sin, that nags us—however gently—when we violate that universal moral code embedded in our psyche. And Isaiah, writing in the context (as we would describe it today) of the Judeo-Christian understanding of morality, almost certainly had in mind as part of that universal moral code, the Ten Commandments, given to Israel amid the thunders of Sinai.

To hearken to those commandments brings peace, as countless millions have discovered through the centuries. Nor can any earthly potion quench the guilt that comes with violating the instructions of a holy God. Even the most hardened criminals cannot bury their guilt. Like spiders, guilt enters into the cottage of the beggar as into the palace of the king.

In a gripping scene in *Macbeth* the famous English playwright gives a vivid, true-to-life picture of the mental havoc guilt can cause. Lady Macbeth has taken the life of King Duncan—who, with his wife, had been an overnight guest in the Macbeth residence—and her mind becomes deranged with guilt. In her nightmare she sees her hand, the hand that had held the dagger, stained with blood; and in anguish she cries out, "Here's the smell of the blood still. All the perfumes of Arabia will not sweeten this little hand. Oh, oh, oh!"[1]

As her condition worsens, her husband summons the doctor who, after examining her, is confronted by him: "How does your patient, Doctor?"

The doctor says, "Not so sick, my lord, as she is troubled with thick-coming fancies that keep her from her rest"—Shakespeare's way of describing the destabilizing specter of chronic guilt.

"Cure her of that," says the anxious Macbeth.

Then, noticing the doctor's uncertainty (as I imagine it), Macbeth cries out in plaintive disbelief, desperate for any possible way that the doctor could rid Lady Macbeth of her plaguing inner trouble. "Canst thou not minister to a mind diseased, pluck from the memory a rooted sorrow," Macbeth implores. Could the doctor not "raze out the written troubles of the brain"? Was there not "some sweet oblivious antidote [to] cleanse the stuffed bosom of that perilous stuff which weighs upon the heart?"

The doctor shakes his head no. "Therein," he says, "the patient must minister to himself."

With this, Macbeth's temper explodes, and he shouts, "Throw physic [meaning medicine] to the dogs, I'll [have] none of it."[2]

But what Macbeth did not know was that no earthly physician could cure the malady crippling his wife in that hour, that no earthly potion could fix her tormented state. And what Macbeth's doctor did not know was that therein patients cannot minister to themselves. But to paraphrase the ancient prophet, there is a balm in Gilead, there is a physician there (see Jer. 8:22). And it's that Physician who says to the troubled, guilt-ridden inhabitants of this wayward planet, "Come now, and let us reason together. . . . Though your sins are like scarlet, they shall be as white as snow; though they are red like crimson, they shall be as wool" (Isa. 1:18, NKJV).

To rephrase the lines of an old song: "What can wash away our guilt? Nothing but the blood of Jesus!"

Seeing It Another Way

Does this mean that those living in compliance with the Ten Commandments are somehow shielded from trouble, from anxiety, from stress?

Clearly, the answer is no. Tragedies and calamities come equally to all people, and our keeping of the Ten Commandments has no direct bearing on our ability to cope with crisis. On the contrary, our adherence to those commandments could even create additional layers of stress as we inwardly question why commandment-keeping folk like us should be subjected to misfortune, disappointment, and calamity.

So what promise does the text offer to people living in compliance with God's will as expressed in the Decalogue?

I think we get a better grasp of the meaning of the text when we understand "commandments" in a broader sense, as including all the counsels of God, especially those we can violate and yet remain in *good and regular standing* in any religious community. Like this one in Isaiah 30:15: "This is what the Sovereign Lord . . . says: 'In repentance and rest is your salvation, in quietness and trust is your strength, but you would have none of it.'" Those seven last words ("but you would have none of it") indicate that, however indirectly phrased, the preceding words (of verse

15) constitute a divine call to repentance and trust—a call to which we often (with impunity) fail to respond, no one but ourselves being aware of our refusal.

Isaiah 26:3, 4 provides another example: "You will keep in perfect peace those whose minds are steadfast, because they trust in you. Trust in the Lord forever, for the Lord, the Lord himself, is the Rock eternal."

To return to God in repentance, to spend time before Him in quiet confidence, to put our trust in Him completely—these are divine requirements, too, right up there with the Ten Commandments in importance, and they permeate the whole of Scripture. To adhere to them is the secret of lasting inner peace.

Ours is the privilege to experience the peace that only God can give—peace like a river. However wild the tempest, however dark the night, however deep the crisis.

---

[1] Shakespeare, *Macbeth*, Act V, scene 1, lines 56, 57.

[2] *Ibid.*, scene 3, lines 37-47.

CHAPTER 9

The Agony and the Ecstasy: From Struggle and Pain to Ultimate Joy

Do you not know that in a race the runners all compete, but only one receives the prize? Run in such a way that you may win it. Athletes exercise self-control in all things; they do it to receive a perishable wreath, but we an imperishable one" (1 Cor. 9:24, 25, NRSV).

As kids, my younger sister and I would go to the home of our older, Roman Catholic cousin to play. I can remember often sitting in the shade of a large tree in the heat of the day listening to him tell us little Anglican kids stories about heaven.

I remember him saying to us: "You will come to two roads." (And he spoke as though that will happen only after we die.) "One road will be paved with gold, strewn with flowers and fruit, enchanting music everywhere. Don't take it," he said. "It leads to hell. The other road," he told us, "will be rough, unpaved, rocky, filled with thorns and briars. Take it," he said. "It leads to heaven."

Our cousin was wrong about that choice coming after death, but he was dead-on in his depiction of the critical alternatives facing each person—*right here and now, in this life*. For the path of the Christian, often beset with struggle, disappointment, and pain, may sometimes amount to downright *agony*. But in the future there's the promise of unspeakable ecstasy when we behold the face of Jesus.

That, basically, is the message of the biblical passage before us—the specter of sacrifice, determination, and struggle, culminating in the heavenly prize.

The View From the Grandstand

I like to think about the life and times of distant civilizations. And one of the favorite regions of my mental wanderings is ancient Greece, land of poets, debaters, philosophers—and (for my purpose here) *athletes*. In my imagination I've often wandered down its ancient streets, gazing up at its beautiful temples, its spectacular monuments. I've sat in the pavilion at Olympus and watched the runners of the ancient Olympics appear for the finals in those famous Games founded more than 2,700 years ago—around the time of Homer, Pericles, and Demosthenes.

Attendance and participation at the Games were at first restricted to Greek citizens, but the passage of time apparently brought a loosening of this limitation. "In the 2nd century A.D., Roman citizenship was extended to everyone within the Roman Empire," a development that saw "the participation of many competitors from outside of Greece in the Olympic games."[1]

Such relaxations in accepted customs are usually centuries in the making, and so it's not inconceivable that Paul in his time may have had opportunity to attend one or more of those famous games. At any rate, the text before us demonstrates a keen acquaintance on his part with Olympic practices, as one would expect of any educated person in the Greco-Roman world.

Paul must have sat there in the ancient stadium, in fact or imagination, and watched the runners appear for the finals. Before the finals, the many elimination contests would have been held in the individual towns and cities throughout the nation.[2] And now the big day has arrived, the event being ushered in by the sound of rousing music and the thunderous cheers of a packed arena.

As each athlete prepares to take the field, the music and the cheering die down as a herald announces the athlete's name, his father's name, and the name of his city. Then the cheering and the music swell again. "Fellow citizens of Greece," cries the herald, announcing the final runner, "here comes Perseus, son of Dionysius, of the city of Sparta." And with this the music and applause rise to earsplitting decibels.

Now they're all lined up; the vast audience is sitting on the edges of their seats, excitement flooding the pavilion. "On your marks!" says the starter, "Get set! *Apite*! [Go!]"[3] And off they go, each sturdy athlete straining every muscle, every fiber of his conditioned body, toward winning the race. Strong legs, so long in training upon Elean fields, are speeding down the track toward the goal. As the competitors prepare for the final dash, pandemonium breaks out in the pavilion. Every man is on his feet.

"Fellow citizens of Greece," the herald bellows from the podium, "we give you Perseus . . . of the city of Sparta—Olympic champion!" And a pavilion of Greek males, a thousand cheering Spartans in the lead, flood the city with a mighty roar of adulation.

The second-century Greek rhetorician and satirist, Lucian, was not scoffing when he described the rush one received at an ancient Olympic encounter: "No-one can describe in mere words the extraordinary . . . pleasure derived from [these athletes] and which you yourself would enjoy if you were seated among the spectators feasting your eyes on the prowess and stamina of the athletes, the beauty and power of their bodies, their incredible dexterity and skill, their invincible strength, their courage, ambition, endurance and tenacity. You would never stop . . . applauding them."[4]

To Seize the Prize

Paul was probably reflecting on experiences such as Lucian described when he wrote the opening lines of the passage before us: "Do you not know that in a race the runners all compete, but only one receives the prize? Run in such a way that you may win it."

Did Paul know that in the Christian race the victory does not go only to the swift? Of course he did. Did he know that in the Christian race the prize goes to *all* who continue to the end? Yes. But his point is that even if everyone may win the Christian prize, as individuals we must run as hard as if only one person could win, and we needed to be that person. "Run *in such a way* that you may win it." Run as vigorously as these Olympian athletes did.

"And everyone who competes for the prize is temperate in all things" (1 Cor. 9:25, NKJV). That translation has given rise to many temperance sermons over the years, but the original sense of the statement is somewhat different. The expression "competes for the prize" is represented by a single word in the Greek: *agonizomai,* bringing to mind English words such as "agony" and "agonize." And the word translated "temperate" in some versions carries the idea of *self-control*, as many contemporary translations render it. Thus we may paraphrase the sentence as "Everyone who *agonizes* (for the victory) *practices self-control* in all things."

Here again the apostle's familiarity with the races comes through. Ten months before the Games began in any given year, the magistrates in the city of Elis (in ancient southern Greece) chose a body of 10 *hellanodikai* (judges), who in turn selected those suitable to begin training for the Games.[5] Under the supervision of these *hellanodikai*, those chosen underwent 10 months of intensive training. Their diet was controlled, their recreation was controlled, their social life was controlled. There was a set time for eating, for sleeping, for bathing, for talking. It was sheer discipline for 10 long months.

At the end of that grueling period, they were taken to the gymnasium, near the race site, for a period of special testing that lasted one additional punishing month,[6] during which they were kept secluded, each athlete in his own cell, not being allowed to see or talk to anyone, so as to guard against bribery. And for the last 15 days, some sources say, their meal consisted chiefly of yogurt and water.

On the morning of the race each athlete took the oath of fair practice,[7] was stripped, then was anointed with oil. They ran naked—no women being allowed into the Games, on pain of being thrown headlong over the Typean rocks.[8] The demanding rigor of preparation behind them, these ancient athletes came to the day of the race charged with almost superhuman powers for the contest.

Struggle for the Mind

Before us lies a race of such stupendous consequence that the Grecian Olympics and their modern counterpart fade into utter insignificance in comparison. Should our spiritual preparation be any less rigorous?

Notice that the Greeks in their training placed emphasis not only on the physical but also—and to a surprising degree—on the mental and psychological disposition of the athlete. The yogurt-and-water treatment was designed, I suspect, to call forth the powers of the mind and discipline the body to respond to the higher impulses lodged within the brain.

It would be dangerous to underestimate the critical importance of the mind in the spiritual struggles we face. The Holy Spirit cannot get through to us via our hands. There are no entry points for the Spirit in our mouths or our nostrils or even our eyes. The only avenue for the Spirit is the mind. Only those fantastically delicate brain cells have the capacity to respond to the signals from the voice of God.

When Dr. Christiaan Barnard of South Africa performed the first human heart transplant back in December 1967, some Christians became alarmed that the psyche of the patient recipient was being compromised, that their personality was being altered, that they were becoming a different individual. But that concern was unwarranted. It's the mind that controls us; it's the mind that "houses" our psyche. And often when the Bible speaks about the heart, it really means the mind.

When those delicate brain cells have been damaged by the consumption of harmful products, by overwork, by lack of adequate rest and exercise; confused by the pervasive prurience of a decadent society; contaminated by our indulgence in the rampant immorality of the neo-pagan culture that surrounds us; poisoned by the fatuous philosophies of pseudoscience, the coarseness and vulgarity of what passes as comedy on contemporary radio and television, the paperback sewage available at every street-corner convenience store, and the rising tide of toxic Internet junk; then these delicate receptor cells become dead to the voice of God.

The stakes are high. Realize it or not, we're caught in a gigantic spiritual struggle, a struggle for the human mind; and Paul finds a parallel in the agonizing physical and mental preparation for those ancient Games.

Most of Paul's athletic-related comments had to do with what's been called the *stade*-race, the major footrace of the ancient Olympics. But we may assume that the apostle also was aware of other significant events at these quadrennial assemblies, not the least of which was the *hoplitodromos*, a race in which athletes did two lengths of the stadium, wearing "helmets on their heads and metal greaves below the knees, and . . . carrying the large round shield that was the main protective device of the Greek infantry soldier, or *hoplite*."[9] According to Plutarch (as reported in Spivey), "the event came last in the competitive sequence . . . in order to emphasize that the ultimate aim of athletics was military prowess."[10]

This connection between athlete and soldier is probably why Paul tended to mix metaphors about the races with that of conflict, struggle, and warfare. The ancient Olympians agonized in competing among themselves. But according to Paul, "our fight is not against any physical enemy: it is against organisations and powers that are spiritual. We are up against the unseen power that controls this dark world, and spiritual agents from the very headquarters of evil" (Eph. 6:12, Phillips). Billions of unfallen beings are looking down upon the contest. Therefore, whatever the cost, whatever the agony, "let us lay aside every weight, and the sin which so easily ensnares us, *and let us run with endurance the race that is set before us*, looking unto Jesus, the author and finisher of our faith" (Heb. 12:1, 2, NKJV).

The Reward

Now, "they do it to receive a perishable wreath, but we an imperishable one."

It's a stark contrast that Paul paints here: on the one hand, *a corruptible wreath*; on the other, *an incorruptible crown*. In our mock footrace at the beginning, Perseus emerged as the Olympic champion. Here's what he got for winning.[11]

1. He received a wreath, a chaplet, a garland, or a crown of sacred olives, taken from the sacred tree, near the temple of Zeus. (Such tokens mean little to us in the twenty-first century, but they were icons to die for in ancient Greece. And in regard to the olives from the sacred tree near Zeus's temple, that was significant, since the Olympics—for many centuries, at least—was intrinsically religious in nature.)
2. The spectators pelted him with flowers and fruit.
3. An elaborate banquet was held in his honor.
4. A statue of him was erected in the hall of fame in the city of Elis.
5. Upon returning to his native city, he did not enter through the city gate. Instead, a breach was made in the city wall, through which his chariot rode, drawn by a team of white horses amid the cheers of the entire city. Dressed in royal purple, the Olympic champion listened to songs and poetry composed in his honor.
6. For the rest of his life he dined at public expense,[12] he was exempted from taxes, and his name was immortalized in the records and annals of his city and the nation.

Judith Swaddling is correct when she says that "the greatest achievement for an athlete in the ancient world was to win the Olympic crown. The material prizes offered at other athletic festivals were insignificant compared to the fame and glory earned by the Olympic victor."[13]

But all these honors Paul regarded as ephemeral, "corruptible," "perishable." And indeed they were. For where now are those white horses and chariots? Where can be found copies of the songs and poetry composed to celebrate these champions? Where to locate those statues in stone, those royal robes of purple, those olive crowns? They've all crumbled into the dust of time. Indeed, "earthquakes and floods [eventually] covered Olympia [itself] with gravel and soil," finally burying the city "beneath 20 feet (6 meters) of earth."[14]

Yes, they did it "to receive a perishable wreath." They agonized for the ephemeral, the temporal, the corruptible. But with no less determination, Paul reached out in another direction for a crown of life that never fades. And at the end of his course he was able to utter the triumphant declamation:

"I have fought the good fight, *I have finished the race,* I have kept the faith. Finally, there is laid up for me the crown of righteousness, which the Lord, the righteous Judge, will give to me on that Day, and not to me only but also to all who have loved His appearing" (2 Tim. 4:7, 8, NKJV).

But before the excitement, before the exultation, before the awesome ecstasy of that thrilling moment, there is the struggle, the pain, the agony. The ancient Olympians did it for Zeus. We do it for Jesus. And we do it *in His strength alone.*

---

[1] "Brief History of the Olympic Games," Nostos: Hellenic Information Society (U.K.), 2000, http://www.nostos.com/olympics/#AncientOlympicGames (in the section: "The Internationalization of the Olympic Games").

[2] Some of the claims I make in this chapter are based on research I did decades ago, which makes it difficult to track down some sources for adequate attribution. I do not consider this critical, however, since my purpose here is that of general illustration, rather than academic precision. I might also note that historians are not all agreed on every detail about the ancient Olympics, and accounts sometimes vary widely.

[3] See Nigel Spivey, *The Ancient Olympics: A History* (Oxford: Oxford University Press, 2004), p. 115; Judith Swaddling, *The Ancient Olympic Games* (Austin, Tex.: University of Texas Press, 1980), p. 48.

[4] Lucian, *Anacharis 12,* cited in Swaddling, p. 79.

[5] See *Encyclopedia Britannica*, 1961 ed., vol. 16, p. 778, s.v. "Olympia"; Swaddling, p. 35.

[6] *Ibid.*

[7] Spivey, p. 78; Swaddling, p. 41.

[8] Pausanias, *Description of Greece,* vol. 6.7, cited in Swaddling, p. 41. "Apparently [however,] this ban applied only to married women, as Pausanias states elsewhere that 'virgins were not refused admission'" (Swaddling, p. 40); cf. Spivey, pp. 119, 120. (Pausanias was a Greek traveler and geographer in the second century A.D.)

[9] Spivey, p. 115.

[10] Spivey, p. 116; cf. Swaddling, p. 44.

[11] Again, my research on these details goes back decades, making it difficult to recapture the sources originally consulted. However, the points I make here are generally known, and several of them might be found distilled in the chapter "Sweet Victory" in Spivey, pp. 125-168.

[12] Swaddling, p. 93.

[13] *Ibid.*

[14] *World Book Encyclopedia,* 1975 ed., vol. 14, p. 565, s.v. "Olympia"; cf. Spivey, pp. 238-248; cf. Swaddling, p. 13.

Chapter 10

Keeping the Sabbath: Valuing God's Gift of Sacred Time

Mouth wide open, I'm sitting in the dentist's chair and listening to the chitchat between him and his assistant. They're talking about a young married couple, the dentist's son and his wife. Apparently, the couple is about to have a baby, and the dentist's assistant wants to know how they're doing.

Assistant: How did your son fare in the recent snowstorm?

Dentist: He failed the test.

A: How so?

D: Well, he didn't get the snow removed till late Sunday.

A: Didn't have a shovel?

D: Yes, he did. But, you know, they're not supposed to remove the snow on Saturday.

A: What?

D: He could have removed it Saturday night, but somehow he didn't. So when I got there Sunday, it had hardened.

A: Well, didn't he have to use the car?

D: They don't drive on Saturdays. I do, but they don't.

A: Wow!

D: I suppose if the baby comes on Saturday, we won't know until sometime Saturday night or Sunday.

A: How so?

D: They don't use the telephone on Saturdays.

A: But how will they get to the hospital?

D: Oh, they can drive in that case because it would be an emergency.

As I listened, I couldn't help thinking how much more liberal we are as Adventists in our Sabbath practices, compared to Orthodox Jews; and (in my thinking) how much more reasonable—and human.

But might there be a flip side to all this?

Pendulum Swings

When Jesus came, He found a Jewish nation riddled with a multitude of human-made Sabbath rules, misguidedly designed to protect the sacred day. While reading in John a while back, I found myself shaking my head as if I'd not read the passage a hundred times before. The story recounted the depressing scene at the Pool of Bethesda, where "a great number of disabled people used to lie—the blind, the lame, the paralyzed" (John 5:1-5). Coming upon the gloomy spectacle, Jesus discovers a man who'd been an invalid 38 years. The Master heals him, then tells him, "Get up! Pick up your mat and walk" (verse 8).

How would the religious leaders react to this astonishing miracle? Would they rejoice to see this erstwhile, wretched man now brimming with radiant health? One might think so. But there was just one problem: the whole joyful, thrilling incident had taken place on Sabbath! "It is the Sabbath," they said to the beaming man, and "the law forbids you to carry your mat. . . . Who is this fellow who told you to pick it up and walk?" (verses 9-12).

Incredible! Instead of being absolutely dumbstruck with wonder and joy, they're looking to kill somebody for breaking one of their own concocted Sabbath rules. Such glaring Sabbath abuse has made us gun-shy about any discussion that involves the question of how one should keep the Sabbath. But wisdom is all about knowing when pendulums have swung too far.

How about a Seventh-day Adventist beginning his or her journey during Sabbath hours in order to be on time for a secular function Saturday night? How about deliberately commencing one's vacation travel on the Sabbath day? How about ball games and other sports on Sabbath afternoon—or even in the morning? I was visiting a church where one of the leaders took about two minutes to announce a basketball game that Saturday night, to commence at 7:45, even though their own bulletin that morning published the sunset time as 7:41.

Other such examples might be strung out endlessly, but that's not the point here. The point is If Jesus came to earth in our time, would His emphasis about Sabbathkeeping be the same? Or would He charge us with doing to this sacred day what the Jews of His time had done to His sacred house, the Temple?

We should welcome all attempts to rescue the Sabbath from legalism and human-made regulations alien to its spirit and purpose. And I'm glad for efforts over the past 50 years or so to develop a theology of the Sabbath that points to the institution's deeper meaning and significance in the modern context. But with scores of thousands of new believers joining the Adventist Church every year, it seems altogether appropriate, from time to time, to focus on the important issue of Sabbathkeeping. My fear is that if we take this vital element for granted, the time will come when our Sabbath observance is no different from the way the majority of Christians keep Sunday.

Sabbath at Sister Davidson's

A young Anglican boy, I'd always known about Adventists in the small community where I grew up, and together with the rest of my family, I despised them. But just before leaving home to enroll in secondary school, I happened to attend some Adventist evangelistic meetings. Deeply impressed, I set out for secondary school; and by sheer coincidence (in retrospect, providence) found myself as a boarder in the home of Sister Susannah Davidson, an Adventist woman of long and prominent standing in her local church. Here I would encounter Sabbathkeeping up close for the first time.

In Sister Davidson's house all family members had their chores come Friday afternoon, working toward the single goal of getting everything done by sundown. By sundown, the house was clean, showers had been taken, Sabbath clothes were ready, the Sabbath meal prepared. And as everyone gathered in the family room for sundown worship, the aroma of freshly baked bread filled the entire house—a mouthwatering reminder that supper was to follow. For someone just getting acquainted with Sabbathkeeping, I couldn't have asked for a better example.

Sabbath was a time for wearing your best, whatever that was. You dressed in a manner that showed you valued the day enough to save the best you had for it. And it was considered a part of good Sabbath practice to come to church smelling fresh. When Ellen White spoke about the baths being taken before Sabbath, I think she was talking against the background of her time, when taking a bath was a major production, with water having to be fetched—likely from a well—and carried into the bathroom. In wintertime, a fire would have been needed to take the chill out. And when you consider larger family sizes in those days, it's not hard to see the need to have these chores cared for before the Sabbath.

The principle behind that standard still holds today, I think. And I find it hard to welcome Sabbath properly without taking a shower first. With a good underarm deodorant, one shower can hold most people through the Sabbath; but for those whose body chemistry demands it, it wouldn't be inappropriate to take a quick shower Sabbath morning, as well. If you'd pardon the indelicacy, Christians should not smell. And Ellen White's admonition about showers should not be used as an excuse for offending the aesthetic sensibilities of other worshippers.

It's at Sister Davidson's that I learned many of the things I now practice automatically in regard to Sabbath: secular magazines and books on my coffee table put away or hidden from plain view, secular radio and television programs off, religious music playing—or just plain quiet filling the space, special food prepared, etc.

I learned that Sabbath is about atmosphere, about a radical change of pace, about finding space for God, about making time for special communion with Him. It's about expelling every intrusion within our power so as to create an environment in which spirituality can strengthen. The songwriter had it right:

"How sweet upon this sacred day,
The best of all the seven,
To cast our earthly thoughts away,
And think of God and heaven!"[1]

Does God Care How We Keep Sabbath?

As we know, the Sabbath had its origin at Creation, when God set the supreme example by resting from His creative work. Later He would make His will explicit in the heart of the Decalogue, enjoining us to "do no work" in this sacred time (see Ex. 20:8-11, NKJV).

It's a 24-hour period, however. We are human beings, and life must go on. So the command to "do no work" calls for some interpretation.

In this connection I accept as relevant the clarification we find in connection with the Feast of Passover, since—as we may logically assume—the rest connected with it (and with the other ancient feasts and observances) was patterned after that of the weekly Sabbath. On both the first and seventh days of the Passover celebration, the people were to "hold a sacred assembly." Then, according to the text, they were to "do no work at all on these days, *except to prepare food for everyone to eat; that is all you may do*" (Ex. 12:16).

Here we see a critical interpretation of the do-no-work stipulation.

The Sabbath is not for fasting; food must be prepared, and that entails some work.

From Exodus 16, however, we get a hint as to the kind of work envisioned here. The people were to collect only so much manna each day, since any surplus went bad overnight. But on Friday they were to gather enough for two days, with no spoilage. Explaining the phenomenon, Moses says, "This is what the Lord commanded: 'Tomorrow is to be a day of sabbath rest, a holy sabbath to the Lord. So bake what you want to bake and boil what you want to boil. Save whatever is left and keep it until morning'" (verse 23). Whether out of stubbornness or curiosity, some people went out on Sabbath in search of the product, "but they found none" (verse 27). Thus God made a clear distinction between the Sabbath and the other days of the week. Exactly what they fixed and how they ate it, we do not know. But according to Exodus 35:3, they were not to "light a fire in any of [their] dwellings on the Sabbath day."

Does this mean that we today should eat cold food on the Sabbath? I once had an experience that showed what it would mean if we answered yes to that question.

As is often the case while on itinerary, I'd not had a proper meal that Friday evening; and breakfast had consisted of what little my hosts had stashed away in the guest apartment cupboards and refrigerator. So all morning I'd been looking forward to lunch, especially after preaching in two different churches before midday—and also because I'd been scheduled for two more sermons in different churches in the afternoon.

Alas, however, lunch was beastly cold—the rice, the potatoes, the entrée, everything. I always try to be flexible, but that day I found it impossible to get things down; so I preached that entire Sabbath hungry.

Is this what God wants? I don't think so.

A good way to understand the passage about not making a fire on the Sabbath is to see it in context. When you try to imagine what it would have looked like in the Israelite camp with the smoke of 100,000 fires covering the encampment, then you see immediately that that was not the atmosphere God wanted for this sacred time. In many places today, on the other hand, the process of producing heat to warm food is as easy as brushing one's teeth. And while I think it's proper, as the ancient Israelites did, to prepare the bulk of our food ahead of Sabbath, I can see no good reason to eat it cold. With our modern conveniences, the effort to warm it up is not much more than what's needed to bring it to the table. Making food palatable is the kind of work implied in Exodus 12:16.

What's needed, I think, is what I'd call *a relaxed carefulness.* The following experience can serve to illustrate the point.

Arriving in the Caribbean on a Thursday evening for a series of speaking appointments back in 2002, I had the good fortune of being located at a beach hotel on the island of Barbados, the first stop on my itinerary. A beach hotel! It sounds exciting. But I've returned from several such situations without ever setting foot on the sand, my hosts' tight schedule seeing to that. But this time, I determined that things would turn out differently.

However, after returning to the hotel early Friday afternoon following my first speaking appointment, I still needed to brush up on four sermons for the weekend, in addition to getting my clothes and other stuff set for Sabbath. So it wasn't until about 5:30 that I felt ready to head to the beach, forgetting that throughout most of the Caribbean the sun religiously goes down between 5:50 and 6:25.

I remember the moment well. Alone in the water (most people preferring to swim when the sun is hot) and watching that big ball of light descending beneath the distant horizon, I literally jumped when it suddenly dawned on me that that was the signal for the beginning of Sabbath! Not one to "go to the beach" on Sabbath, I was instinctively prepared to rush away. But just as suddenly a voice inside me (I believe the Spirit's) said: *Just calm down, Roy! Where do you think you are? You're in God's own big pond at the end of a busy week and a hectic day! What better place to welcome the holy Sabbath?*

So there I was, all alone and in my swimwear, singing, "Day is dying in the west," my voice bouncing off the water back to me, almost as if I had celestial company. It's a Sabbath welcome I shall never forget!

How would you have reacted? If I'd have been in the same location the following Friday, that certainly wouldn't have been the time I would choose for the beach. But under the circumstances, God tried to teach me the art of relaxed carefulness.

God's intention is that the Sabbath should be a day of renewal. In a passage filled with poetic beauty, Isaiah paints a picture of the blessings that await all who honor God in the context of this sacred day: "If you keep your feet from breaking the Sabbath and from doing as you please on my holy day, if you call the Sabbath a delight and the Lord's holy day honorable, and if you honor it by not going your own way and not doing as you please or speaking idle words, then you will find your joy in the Lord, and I will cause you to ride on the heights of the land and to feast on the inheritance of your father Jacob" (Isa. 58:13, 14).

Comparing this text to its sister passage in Jeremiah 17:24-27, I take it to mean that on the Sabbath I should channel my activities and thoughts in a different direction than on other days of the week, as befitting the sacredness of these special hours. If I'm a merchant, I don't do sales on Sabbath. If I'm a schoolteacher, I don't do class on Sabbath. If I'm an electrician, I don't string wires on Sabbath. If I'm an attorney, I don't do cases on Sabbath. If I'm a student, I don't do books on Sabbath. And if I'm a pastor, a physician, or a nurse, then Sabbath brings a modification, though not necessarily a complete stoppage, of my work.

There are exceptions, of course—for emergencies or special situations. When disaster strikes, for example, you respond in whatever way seems appropriate: you fix a tire, you cook, you haul wood, you dig ditches, you build a house, you bake bread, you do whatever is needed in the particular crisis. But when under regular circumstances (and to prove a point), we deliberately single out the Sabbath as the time to paint the house of Jane Doe, the elderly woman down the street, or to cut her grass—things that could well wait till Sunday or even Wednesday—then something's wrong with that picture.

Here in Isaiah, God is saying that if I'm careful to observe the Sabbath His way, then He will bless me with a whole bundle of good things I don't even fully understand—such as feeding me with "the heritage of Jacob" (Isa. 58:14, KJV) and all that rich stuff.

Adventists, especially in the industrialized world, are awfully busy during the week, and so they tend to pack a lot of activity into the Sabbath hours. But we should always aim to free up the Sabbath from all unnecessary clutter. One of the best Sabbath afternoons I've ever spent was on the island of Tobago in the Caribbean, when the young people planned a relaxed youth meeting and vesper service in a coconut field down by the seaside. As the big, red sun dipped behind the horizon, its golden afterglow filling the western sky with beauty, the evocative words of Henry de Fluiter flowed out in grateful song, blending with the sound of the lapping waves before us, and reminding us of that glorious day to which every Sabbath points:

"Over yonder, down by the crystal sea,
Over yonder, there's where I long to be,

No more sorrow, toil, grief, nor care,
In that homeland bright and fair,
Over, over there."[2]
What wonderful Sabbaths with Jesus when we get there!

Postscript: A Testimony

It was high school—senior high—a place with a reputation to live up to. The Latin teacher poured it on. The chemistry professor demanded his pound of flesh. And so also did those who taught algebra and geometry and trigonometry. Based on the workload, each teacher seemed to feel as if his or her class were the only one you had.

So here was this country lad, struggling to make good. My head felt crowded, congested—as if nothing else could get in. Wasn't a headache, just a heavy dullness of the mind. And it became a pattern.

Then I met Jesus. And those who spoke to me about Him also told about the Sabbath.

Sabbath! I still remember thinking, *Sacrifice an entire day of study while my classmates press ahead? How can I ever compete?*

But gradually, in His own gentle way, the Lord made things clear to me: the remedy for my congested head lay not in the drive to compete but in the call to disconnect. To disconnect from the frantic pace, the rush for things, the scramble to succeed. And to connect—to love, to hope, to peace. To find rest—of body, of mind, of soul—in Jesus. That's Sabbath.

When I discovered it, my head cleared up. My burdens rolled away.

Sabbath. It's not our Savior. But it calls us to the One who said, "Come to me, all you who are weary and burdened, and I will give you rest" (Matt. 11:28).

---

[1] *The Church Hymnal* (Washington, D.C.: Review and Herald Pub. Assn., 1941), no. 458.

[2] *The Seventh-day Adventist Hymnal* (Hagerstown, Md.: Review and Herald Pub. Assn., 1985), no. 431.

Chapter 11

Singing Our Songs: Tapping the Awesome Power of Music

Following family worship one Friday evening, I asked our daughter Kim to play hymn number 648 from *The Seventh-day Adventist Hymnal*[1]—a piece that had been percolating in my head ever since I first heard it sung in our local church during a Memorial Day service. I'd instantly fallen in love with it, and as I sat there on the floor of our family room that evening listening to its majestic melody on the piano, I felt as if transported to another world.

Preachers and worship leaders should understand the power of music, the effect a certain melody can have on particular individuals sitting in the pews before them and how different those individuals can be in experience, temperament, culture, and taste. In regard to taste, for instance, neither my daughter nor her mom (who was present) cared a thing about the piece that so excited me that evening—an excitement that would grow even deeper because of the following tragic event.

"She's Dead!"

My wife, Celia, and I had been vacationing in the United Kingdom at the end of August 1997. We'd spent the Sabbath in Scotland, returning to London late Saturday night. Sunday would be our last full day in the British capital, and notwithstanding the late-night arrival from Edinburgh, we arose early Sunday morning, not wanting to waste a single hour of that final day. Going down for breakfast at the little Adventist-run bed-and-breakfast where we stayed, we found those who'd preceded us to the table solemn-faced around the television set in the dining room. "She's dead," they said as we arrived. "Princess Diana is dead, killed in a Paris auto accident."

Our entire plans for that final Sunday suddenly changed as we joined tens of thousands of mourners paying final tribute to the fallen royal icon at her Kensington Palace home in West London.

Back in the United States, as I watched a recording of the funeral, I heard the very song I'd asked my daughter to play that Friday evening, embellished by the great organ and choir of Westminster Abbey. A favorite of the princess, the piece (by Sir Cecil Spring-Rice) took on new meaning for me as one of the most powerful songs in our hymnal.

Its first stanza is a pledge of loyalty to country, loyalty anchored in love—"the [kind of] love," the hymn says, "that makes undaunted the final sacrifice." But it's stanza 2 that brings it all home for me, pointing to something far beyond all earthly loyalties. With one line modified in *The SDA Hymnal* to make it more in sync with Scripture, it reads:

"And there's another country, I've heard of long ago,
Most dear to them that love her, most great to them that know;
We may not count her armies, we may not see her King;
Her fortress is a faithful heart, her pride is suffering;
And one by one and fervently we pray for her increase,
And her ways are ways of gentleness and all her paths are peace."[2]

The power of a hymn does not lie solely in its lyrics. Only when set to music do those lyrics become fully loaded with emotive intensity to reach our inmost souls. This means that you're catching less than 50 percent of the force of the words just quoted if you're unfamiliar with the tune.[3]

And my central point in this chapter is that we should try to learn our hymns and be able to sing our songs . . . as much as possible.[4]

How I Got This Burden

My Sabbath morning message in one particular church was to be on the practical aspects of the sanctuary doctrine—on the comfort, protection, and power that flow out from that heavenly place where Jesus ministers for us. So in response to the request for bulletin information, I chose number 527 (*The SDA Hymnal*) for the opening hymn:

"From every stormy wind that blows,
From every swelling tide of woes,
There is a calm, a sure retreat;
'Tis found beneath the mercy seat."

The information supplied, I arrived Sabbath morning with great expectation, looking forward to the spiritual and emotional lift from the congregational singing of that powerful song. But as I sat there on the rostrum, the leader of the praise team came up to whisper in my ear that they didn't know the hymn I'd chosen.

"Don't know it?" I whispered back incredulously, thinking to myself, *So why am I learning this only now?*

"No, we don't. Do you have another choice?"

Typically I'd spend as much as a half hour going through the hymnal, searching for just the right song to match my message. So you'll understand that the last place I'd want to be doing this would be while sitting on the rostrum waiting to speak, with all kinds of last-minute things going through my mind.

"How about number 477?" I eventually said, " 'Come, Ye Disconsolate.' " *It's a good substitute,* I thought. But they didn't know it either.

I mentioned one more. No, they also didn't know it.

"OK," I said finally, "just choose something."

On another occasion, I'd chosen as the opening song that great hymn by Charles Wesley "And Can It Be?" (no. 198), with "O for a Thousand Tongues to Sing" (no. 250) as a backup. Arriving for the Sabbath morning appointment, I was surprised to notice that neither hymn was listed in the program. Instead, they'd chosen "In Christ There Is No East nor West" (no. 587). It takes only a moment to see the huge thematic and emotional gap between my choices and what we ended up singing that day. It can dampen a preacher's mood.

Such experiences have given rise to the burden I now carry on this subject. For me, the hymn selected does not stand on its own. It should complement the preacher's message as closely as possible.

Singing It Right

In some cases the congregation might know the selected piece yet come up short in its execution. One example: With an upcoming preaching appointment occupying my mind, I attended a Sabbath service that closed with the old hymn "Never Part Again" (no. 449). It's a powerful piece when done right—and they did it just right that day! They had "fun" with the song, and one could tell that every line was hitting a spiritual spot in the congregation. All heaven broke loose as they came to the dramatic chorus for the final time:

"What! Never part again? No, never part again,
What! Never part again? No, never part again,
And soon we shall with Jesus reign,
And, never, never part again."

It was the kind of experience that makes a congregation break out in amens after they themselves have sung the hymn. And in the midst of all that inspiration I decided, *That'll be the closing song when I speak in a few weeks. I want to hear it again!*

But what a surprise I was in for! The song director, the pianist, and the congregation found themselves on different planets as the song proceeded, thanks in large part to the song director, who was completely at sea on the timing—and that's a song for which you'd better get the timing right!

Congregational singing, when done right, has a powerful effect on both preacher and people. On the island of Tobago in the Caribbean, I had occasion to select the same hymn mentioned previously, the one by Charles Wesley ("And Can It Be?"). And it was as if that camp meeting crowd had been waiting to sing the piece the entire year and now they got their chance. I'd never heard it done with greater spirit! It so choked me up that I had to step away from the rostrum to pull myself together. You could feel God's living power in the room.

In yet another instance the evangelistic crowd was in the midst of song service as conference president James Daniel and I arrived for the meeting on the tiny island of Bequia, off the coast of St. Vincent, in the eastern Caribbean. "Watch, Ye Saints" (no. 598) was the song in progress at the time, backed up by piano, synthesizer, bass guitar, and whatever other instruments they had. As the congregation launched into the chorus of the piece, "Lo! He comes, lo! Jesus comes," you got the sense that if you were to step outside the tent that very moment, you'd actually see Jesus returning with His angels in the evening sky! It was powerful stuff—full-throttle from the belly!

Something happens when we do it right!

It would be fun to "walk" through the hymnal, sharing favorites and telling what they each mean to us. And there's the added dimension that comes from knowing the background of our hymns.[5] To know the story behind George Matheson's "O Love That Wilt Not Let Me Go" (no. 76) or John Newton's "Amazing Grace" (no. 108) or John Bowring's "In the Cross of Christ I Glory" (no. 237) is to sing these songs with deeper understanding and heightened enthusiasm.[6]

There's Power in It

The Bible emphasizes the importance of music and musicians in corporate worship. The ancient musicians, it says in one place, "stayed in the rooms of the temple and were exempt from other duties because they were responsible for the work day and night" (1 Chron. 9:33)—as many as 4,000 of them (see 1 Chron. 23:5; cf. 2 Chron. 29:25)! They needed to be "skillful" at their task (1 Chron. 15:19-22; cf. 1 Chron. 25:1, 6, 7). During the dedication of the Jerusalem Temple, as the musicians unleashed their cymbals, harps, and lyres, "accompanied by 120 priests sounding trumpets" (can you picture that!) and the choir "[raising] their voices in praise to the Lord[,] . . . the temple of the Lord was filled with a cloud, and the priests could not perform their service because of the cloud, for the glory of the Lord filled the temple of God" (2 Chron. 5:12-14).

There's power in music, in singing. As they emerged from their hair-raising Red Sea experience, the first thing Israel did was sing (Ex. 15); at a critical time in Israel, it was the choir that led the nation's army into battle (2 Chron. 20:20-22); under severe discomfort in a Philippian jail, Paul and Silas broke out into songs at midnight—shaking the ground, so to speak, and leading to the conversion of the jailer and his family (Acts 16:25-31); martyrs across the centuries sang as they faced death head-on; the American slaves, steeped in religion, survived by singing; and who does not know the power of "A Mighty Fortress" (no. 506), the "Battle Hymn of the Reformation"?[7]

We need to sing our songs with greater passion. Adventist musicians should compose new songs, new hymns—about grace, about the Second Coming, about the Holy Spirit, the Resurrection, the Sabbath, and the other great doctrines of our faith—serious songs, "sing-able" songs, songs that touch the soul.

There's something strange about a roomful of grown men and women opening their mouths and making sounds together. But the psychology of it is evident. It solidifies people, creates unity, strengthens resolve, brings comfort, deepens assurance, enhances hope. We do it for the rush it gives, the goose bumps it creates, the confidence it produces.

Before launching into some of what he called "the good old hymns" at one of his concerts, Adventist singer Wintley Phipps made a statement worth repeating: "When you come down to the final moments of your life, you don't want no ditties. You want songs with substance." And the piece he presented following those remarks said it all:

"When peace, like a river, attendeth my way,
When sorrows like sea billows roll—
Whatever my lot, Thou hast taught me to say,
It is well, it is well with my soul."[8]

The story behind that song[9] helps us brace for whatever life may throw at us, while we look forward to that stupendous day when, coming out of great tribulation, we shall join God's people from around the world and across the centuries upon the sea of glass to sing the Song of Moses and the Lamb. What an awesome moment that will be!

---

[1] Referred to hereafter as "*The SDA Hymnal*," "the hymnal," "our hymnal," "the hymnbook," etc. Numbers in parentheses throughout the chapter refer to hymn numbers in this work.

[2] The original line reads, "And soul by soul and silently her shining bounds increase"—much more elegant than the substitute in our hymnal; but it could give the impression that "souls" go one by one to heaven at death.

[3] If the video is still up on YouTube, why not give a listen to the actual rendition by the Westminster Abbey choir at Princess Diana's funeral? (http://www.youtube.com/watch?v=LmeQ_M7fPMw&feature=related)

[4] The expression "singing our songs" should not convey the idea that we should individually *like* each song in the hymnal. In fact, if it were left to me, some of the hymns included would never have made it in. But we ought to do the best with what we have. Moreover, the "our" in "singing our songs" does not refer only to the hymnal widely used in North America (where I happen to live), but rather to the official hymnal wherever you reside in the world. And every official hymnal should take pains to reflect the multicultural, multiethnic reality wherever the church operates.

[5] For brief background stories surrounding the hymns in our hymnal, see Wayne Hooper and Edward E. White, *Companion to the Seventh-day Adventist Hymnal* (Hagerstown, Md.: Review and Herald Pub. Assn., 1988).

[6] Incidentally, whether we're into contemporary music or classical or gospel, or whatever, we should remember that our minds have the capacity to appreciate a wide variety of genres. We need not restrict ourselves exclusively to a single category.

[7] See Hooper and White, p. 488.

[8] *The Seventh-day Adventist Hymnal*, no. 530.

[9] Horatio Spafford wrote the song while grieving for his four young daughters, whose ship went down in the Atlantic, off the coast of Newfoundland (see Hooper and White, pp. 504, 505).

Chapter 12

Service in a World Gone Mad: From the Drive for Money, Fame, and Power

The spring of 2000 saw the birth (on CBS) of reality television in the United States, with the popular show called *Survivor* leading the way. In a venom-laden speech in the series' final episode, participant Susan Hawk lambasted fellow contestant Kelly Wiglesworth for what she saw as Kelly's deceptive conniving, which she felt had robbed her of the grand prize of $1 million.

Speaking to Kelly in front of fellow participants and millions of television viewers, Susan spat out the cutting words that told exactly how she felt: "I'll shake your hand and I'll go on from here. But if I were ever to pass you along in life again and you were laying *[sic]* there dying of thirst, I would not give you a drink of water. I would let the vultures take you and do whatever they want with you with no ill regrets."

Politically incorrect in the extreme, those sentiments represent, nevertheless, an element of Western culture that is more widespread than most of us are ready to admit. And the question is Have Christians bought into that ethos? Is the ideal that puts others first dead? Has the whole world, including us, gone mad with greed, with the lust for celebrity and power?

Jesus addressed this issue in one of His admonishments to His disciples. "You know that the rulers of the Gentiles lord it over them, and their high officials exercise authority over them. Not so with you. Instead, whoever wants to become great among you must be your servant, and whoever wants to be first must be your slave—just as the Son of Man did not come to be served, but to serve, and to give his life as a ransom for many" (Matt. 20:25-28).

Against the background of this passage I'd like to reflect on service in the twenty-first century under three categories: the motive, the Model, and the mystery.

The Motive

I read a sad story out of Paris back in March of 2003 about a three-star French chef named Bernard Loiseau. For the French, as perhaps the whole world knows, the preparation of food is a work of art, top-rated French chefs enjoying a prestige within the country equal to that of movie stars.

According to the story, Loiseau, who'd begun his work as a lowly cook down in the back of the kitchen, had worked his way up over the years, demonstrating, the story said, "an obsessive dedication" to the intricacies of his vocation. With that kind of focus he eventually grew "into one of the most celebrated masters of fine cuisine in the world."[1]

The French people went gaga over him. And year after year, as far back as 1991, his flagship restaurant southeast of Paris was given the highest rating—three-stars—from the most prestigious restaurant-evaluating agency in France. For Loiseau it was "the fulfillment of [a] lifetime quest for recognition," the report said. He became "the only chef [in the country] whose business traded on the French stock exchange." He published books, he made regular television appearances, he produced a frozen food line, etc. In short, Loiseau had become a high-profile celebrity in the country.[2]

But in late February of 2003 tragedy struck. It happened after the second most prestigious restaurant-rating agency in France dropped his standing (in their system) from 19 to 17 on a scale of 20. Loiseau felt crushed, devastated. Alone at home one day, he put a gun to his head.

I found the incident instructive for us as Christians—especially for Christian pastors and leaders—whose raison d'être, whose very reason for existence, is ministry, service. For here, in Loiseau's case, the sheer joy of service had become twisted, eclipsed by a preoccupation with recognition, popularity, and power.

And I found the incident doubly significant when I read the comment Loiseau's wife made on French television in the wake of her husband's suicide. She said, "All these people, all these exceptional beings who give you the impression of so much assurance, they are all very fragile. They all have such strong moments of doubt."[3]

I'm talking here about motive, about the internal force that drives us and determines the quality of our service in the eyes of God. And I'm saying that if we're to be true servants in a world gone mad with egotism, selfishness, and greed, then it's critical that we each take careful stock of our own motives, stopping long enough to ask the candid question *Why am I doing this?*

It's a question particularly relevant to Christians and, even more so, to Christian leaders. In a world scrambling after money, power, glamour, and fame, why would a bunch of men and women choose a vocation in which they're sometimes belittled, often maligned, and almost always underpaid?

You may have noticed that not a lot of young people are beating down the doors to enter the area of full-time Christian service. Often more lucrative professions beckon. When NBC Television some years ago advertised for its upcoming show *The Apprentice* (with Donald Trump), they needed only 16 participants. But a whopping 215,000 young people applied! For these young folk, that's where the action is. And no wonder; the grand prize was a position as president of a Trump company, with a starting salary of $250,000.[4]

It would be very easy for us to conclude that as Christians our motives are better, purer. After all, we're not in this thing for the money! But while that may be true for many of us, it's also true, as the explosive book *Who Watches? Who Cares?*[5] points out, that the pull of money has not been unknown among us.

Besides, there is something equally as beguiling as money, if not more so. And that something is power. I've always been surprised by the intense struggle among Adventists, and among other Christians too, for recognition; the jockeying to become the biggest fish in this little pond of ours called the church—with some of us, like crabs in a barrel (to change the figure), shamelessly—and sometimes viciously—scrambling over the backs of others to the top. I've seen it.

But in the words of Oliver Wendell Holmes, Sr.: "The noblest service comes from nameless hands. And the best servant does his work unseen." And here's this from Ellen G. White: "Not the great things which every eye sees and every tongue praises does God account most precious. The little duties cheerfully done, the little gifts which make no show, and which to human eyes may appear worthless, often stand highest in His sight."[6]

When I think of Christians of the recent past who have abandoned themselves in selfless service to humanity, one name shoots up above all the rest: Mother Teresa. In this Christian woman we see an example, par excellence, of what theologians call "incarnational ministry," *ministry in the trenches.* Few remember anymore that she was a native of Macedonia. And it matters very little to the bulk of us that she was a Roman Catholic. The one thing that's captured our imagination was her loving ministry for the poor and underprivileged of Calcutta, her total dedication to their welfare. And I would hazard a guess that of the billions of people around the world who've heard of her, only a fraction of them know that she was not Indian, so totally did she identify herself with the people she served.

And in a prayer I understand she offered daily, we get an insight into the motive that propelled her:

"Deliver me, O Jesus: / From the desire of being loved / From the desire of being honored / From the desire of being praised / From the desire of being preferred . . . / From the desire of being consulted / From the desire of being approved / From the desire of being popular. / Deliver me, O Jesus: / From the fear of being humiliated / From the fear of being despised / From the fear of being rebuked / . . . From the fear of being forgotten / From the fear of being wronged / From the fear of being treated unfairly / From the fear of being suspected / And, Jesus, grant me the grace / To desire that others might be more loved than I / That others might be more esteemed than I / That in the opinion of the world, others may increase and I decrease / That others may be chosen and I set aside / That others may be preferred to me in everything."[7]

The overriding motive that drove Mother Teresa's selfless service was *humility*. And that same motive should define our witness today.

The Model

It would not be difficult to twist what Jesus said in the Matthew passage cited above. He says that "whoever wants to be first must be your slave" (Matt. 20:27). I can imagine someone saying, "So *that's* how it's done!—*the Christ-sanctioned way to the top!* I humble myself; play the role of servant; people take notice; then, voila, I'm catapulted to the top. If that's the price I must pay to reach the highest place, I'll do it—yes, I'll do it!"

But almost as if Jesus foresaw how His words might be distorted, He placed Himself at the very heart of the passage, modeling, as it were, the meaning of the admonition: "And whoever wants to be first must be your slave—*just as the Son of Man did not come to be served, but to serve, and to give His life*" (verses 27, 28).

It's the diametrical opposite of the attitude that permeates our culture today. In his immortal classic *Paradise Lost* John Milton insightfully captures the outlook of the fallen angel, an outlook that also has bedeviled us since the Fall. Says Lucifer as he's cast unrepentant from heaven: "Better to reign in Hell than serve in Heaven."[8]

How aptly that posture characterizes the mood of our times!

On Sunday, February 4, 1968, in Atlanta, Martin Luther King, Jr., preached a sermon that has now become famous: "The Drum Major Instinct."[9] The drum major instinct, King said, refers to the impulse in all of us for attention, the "desire to be out front, . . . to lead the parade, . . . to be first."

Surprisingly, he said, Jesus did not condemn His disciples for having that attitude (and you will notice that when you read the passage). Instead, He attempted to transform their concept of greatness. "If you want to be important—wonderful. If you want to be recognized—wonderful. If you want to be great—wonderful. But recognize that he who is greatest among you shall be your servant."[10]

"[This] new definition of greatness," King said, ". . . means that everybody can be great, because everybody can serve. You don't have to have a college degree to serve. You don't have to make your subject and your verb agree to serve. You don't have to know about Plato and Aristotle to serve. You don't have to know Einstein's theory of relativity to serve. . . . You only need a heart full of grace, a soul generated by love. And *you* can be that servant."[11]

Continuing his message—and almost as if he had premonitions of his impending death—then just two months away—he said: "Every now and then I think about my own death and I think about my own funeral. . . . And . . . I ask myself, 'What is it that I would want said?' "

He continued, "If you get somebody to deliver the eulogy, tell them . . . not to mention that I have a Nobel Peace Prize—that isn't important. Tell them not to mention that I have three or four hundred other awards—that's not important. Tell them not to mention where I went to school."

But, he said, "I'd like somebody to mention that day that Martin Luther King, Jr., tried to give his life serving others. . . . [That he] tried to love somebody. . . . [That he tried] to feed the hungry. . . . [That he tried] to clothe those who were naked. . . . [That he tried] to visit those who were in prison. I want you to say that [he] tried to love and serve humanity."

He then added, "Yes, if you want to say that I was a drum major, say that I was a drum major for justice. Say that I was a drum major for peace. I was a drum major for righteousness. And all of the other shallow things will not matter."[12]

Powerful sentiments—and totally in line with the Model of Galilee, who came, not to *be served,* but *to serve,* and to give His life a ransom for many.

Service was the cornerstone of Jesus' life. Two passages in the Gospels, both in Matthew, capture for me the intense passion of Jesus most succinctly, and I'm always looking for an excuse to mention them: According to Matthew 4:23-25, "Jesus went throughout Galilee, teaching . . . , proclaiming the good news . . . , and healing. . . . News about him spread all over Syria, and people brought to him all who were ill . . . , suffering . . ., demon-possessed . . . , paralyzed; and he healed them. Large crowds from Galilee, the Decapolis, Jerusalem, Judea and the region across the Jordan followed him." Then Matthew 9:35, 36, paralleling parts of the previous passage, comes to an end with an added point in big, bold letters: "But when He saw the multitudes, *He was moved with compassion for them*" (verse 36, NKJV).

Moved with compassion!

Across the centuries, many notable Christians have made His life a model for their own—among them, Albert Schweitzer. Brilliant philosopher, eminent physician, competent musician, accomplished theologian, Schweitzer could have chosen the path of fame and comfort in his native Europe. But instead he elected to give more than half a century of his life as a medical missionary to (then) French Equatorial Africa. I read somewhere that his first consulting room at the hospital he founded in Lambaréné, deep in the African rainforest (in what is now the country of Gabon), was a chicken coop. He gave his life in service to some of the poorest humans on the planet, keeping ever in front of him the matchless Model of Galilee.

And in a cryptic, haunting passage at the end of his famous book *The Quest of the Historical Jesus*, he commends the Savior to all who'd care to listen: "He comes to us as One unknown, without a name, as of old, by the lake-side, He came to those men who knew Him not. He speaks to us the same word: 'Follow thou me!' and sets us to the tasks which He has to fulfil for our time. He commands. And to those who obey Him, whether they be wise or simple, He will reveal Himself in the toils, the conflicts, the sufferings which they shall pass through in His fellowship, and, as an ineffable mystery, they shall learn in their own experience Who He is."[13]

Those poignant words from Schweitzer lead naturally to my final point:

The Mystery

I will never understand how it is that a participant in a game show could rake in $1 million, while a veteran in the armed forces who has served his or her country in some of the most dangerous places on earth, risking life and limb (and sometimes coming home without the latter), finds himself or herself jobless and homeless on the street; how fat-cat bank executives can walk away with hundreds of millions of dollars in their pockets, while a hardworking widow with three children loses her home to foreclosure, with all her belongings thrown out on the sidewalk by the county sheriff.

What kind of society is that? Today the aim of altogether too many companies and CEOs is to jip the public while raking in billions—and they never seem to have enough! I read the papers, watch the *Evening News*, see the gross inequities and injustices, and it makes me want to scream with outrage.

Perhaps it was an inner sense of outrage not altogether dissimilar from mine that led the likes of Mother Teresa, her noble service notwithstanding, to experience "forty-five years of inner emptiness, feeling 'neither joy, nor love, nor light . . . [living as if] on a darkling plain.' "[14]

That's where mystery comes in. Mystery gives us the insight to transcend our frustrations over the inequities, exploitations, and injustices all around us, reminding us that this world is not all there is. Mystery points to a *plus ultra* (to borrow a Latin expression), to something beyond, something beyond the things of time.[15] Without that vision, we can go berserk, as happened to the gifted eighteenth-century English clergyman and satirist, Jonathan Swift.

In a scathing satire entitled *Gulliver's Travels*, Swift tells how Gulliver, on a world expedition, was cast ashore on an unknown island by buccaneers, pirates, whom he'd picked up in Barbados and the Leeward Islands. And in a remarkable passage describing the idyllic conditions on that island, Swift was indirectly lambasting the degenerate condition of contemporary English society as he knew it. On this island (he puts words in Gulliver's mouth), there was no "physician to destroy my body, nor lawyers to ruin my fortune." No pickpockets, no politicians, no murderers, no robbers, no cheating shopkeepers or mechanics, no drunkards, no prostitutes, no scoundrels.[16]

Swift was so totally fed up and disgusted with the decadence of contemporary English society that he lost sight of the mystery, lost sight of God's transcendent future, and ended his days in an empty room mentally deranged.

By contrast, Martin Luther King, Jr., equally outraged by many things in the society around him, never lost that sense of mystery. Down in Memphis in support of garbage collectors, and with threats and forebodings of death pressing in upon him, he said to a local congregation the last night of his life: "Like anybody, I would like to live a long life. . . . But I'm not concerned about that now. I just want to do God's will. And He's allowed me to go up to the mountain. And I've looked over, and I've seen the Promised Land [that's mystery]. . . . And so I'm happy tonight. I'm not worried about anything. I'm not fearing any man. Mine eyes have seen the glory of the coming of the Lord."[17]

From the human standpoint, King's life came to a tragic end; but given his deep sense of mystery, as suggested in the words just cited, his end was a glorious one.

While visiting the Richard Nixon Library in Yorba Linda, California, I came across a favorite quotation of the former president from the ancient Greek philosopher Sophocles: "One must wait until the evening to see how splendid the day has been."

I had reason to think about that quotation a short time later when I came to one particularly touching paragraph in a book I was reading, a paragraph about William Manchester, the famous and prolific British writer, and author of the well-respected Winston Churchill biography.

Manchester, if I remember the story correctly,[18] had by then suffered two strokes, leaving his last book on Churchill unfinished. The author I was reading visited Manchester in his home and asked the famous writer whether he intended to complete the Churchill project. Manchester responded sadly, "I can write no more. All I can do now is enjoy my grandchildren the best I can, and wait for the end."

"One must wait until the evening to see how splendid the day has been"? Tell that, Sophocles, to William Manchester as he brooded over his life, helplessly awaiting the end. Tell it to former U.S. president Ronald Reagan as he vegetated under the ravages of Alzheimer's disease. Tell it to the folk sitting in senior citizens' homes all across the planet, confused shells of their former selves.

Correction, Sophocles, you had it wrong. One must wait until the *morning* to see how splendid the day has been. That's what mystery is about, in the context I'm using it here. "Mystery" implies there's *more beyond*, that there's something better to look forward to—in the *morning*! Said the blind Helen Keller: "For three things I thank God every day of my life: thanks that he has vouchsafed me knowledge of his works; deep thanks that he has set in my darkness the lamp of faith; deep, deepest thanks that I have another life to look forward to—a life joyous with light and flowers and heavenly song."[19]

That's the idea of *plus ultra*, the sense that there's more beyond, the concept of mystery. And it begs us, in the midst of all our service and the frustrations that sometimes come with it—or in the midst of all the pomp and trappings that often accompany service in the higher echelons of society—to never forget what's most important. That the greatest sacrifice, in the words of the ancient prophet, is "to act justly and to love mercy and to walk humbly with [our] God" (Micah 6:8).

The year was 1897, and it was Queen Victoria's Diamond Jubilee. The procession left Buckingham Palace with Queen Victoria riding in a decorated horse-drawn carriage, the route lined with tens of thousands of cheering citizens. The steel-lined boots of hundreds and hundreds of London bobbies clicked to attention, their polished rifles at their breasts, as group after group of important dignitaries passed by in parade along King William Street. Military men, officials of the British Admiralty, Indian princes on horseback, high-ranking officers of state, and members of the English clergy moved past in solemn dignity, under the stirring strains of military music, amid the tumult and the shouting of 100,000 voices in praise to Britannia.[20]

Meanwhile, in a house on the north end of London, a man by the name of Rudyard Kipling, on the urging of friends, recovered from the wastebasket, where he had discarded it, a poem, a commentary on the resplendent jubilee celebrations just ended. It read:

"The tumult and the shouting dies—
The Captains and the Kings depart—
Still stands Thine ancient sacrifice,
An humble and a contrite heart.
Lord God of Hosts, be with us yet,
Lest we forget—lest we forget!"

Serving in a world gone mad. To do it effectively, we must carefully examine our *motive*, keep our eyes fixed on our shining *Model*, and ask God to embed within our psyche the *mystery* of a reality beyond the things of time.

---

[1] Keith B. Richburg, "Did Ratings Slide Kill a Great Chef of Europe? Top Cooks Cite Guide in Apparent Suicide," Washington *Post*, Feb. 26, 2003, p. C1.

[2] *Ibid.*

[3] *Ibid.*

[4] *TV Week*, Jan. 4-10, 2004, p. 6.

[5] Douglas Hackleman, *Who Watches? Who Cares?: Misadventures in Stewardship* (Morrison, Colo.: Members for Church Accountability, Inc., 2008).

[6] E. G. White, *The Desire of Ages*, p. 615.

[7] See http://advaharma.wordpress.com/deliver-me-oh-jesus-mother-theresas-prayer/.

[8] John Milton, *Paradise Lost* (London: New English Library, 1961), book 1, line 263.

[9] "Martin Luther King, Jr., "The Drum Major Instinct," sermon, Feb. 4, 1968, Martin Luther King, Jr., Research and Education Institute, Stanford University, http://mlk-kpp01.stanford.edu/index.php/encyclopedia/documentsentry/doc_the_drum_major_instinct/.

[10] *Ibid.*

[11] *Ibid.* (Italics supplied.)

[12] *Ibid.*

[13] Albert Schweitzer, *The Quest of the Historical Jesus* (New York: Macmillan Pub. Co., Inc., 1968), p. 403.

[14] Michael Novak, *No One Sees God: The Dark Night of Atheists and Believers* (New York: Doubleday, 2008), p. 1.

[15] In olden times the Pillars of Hercules (the name given in antiquity to the two prominent rock formations near the Straits of Gibraltar) marked "the edge of the then known world. According to mythology the pillars bore the warning *Nec plus ultra* ('. . . nothing farther beyond'), serving as a warning to sailors and navigators to go no farther." However, as navigation broke the bounds of those pillars and an expansive world came into view, the "Nec" was dropped, so to speak, leaving only "plus ultra," as Europe came to realize that there really was much more beyond that point. See http://en.wikipedia.org/wiki/Plus_ultra_(motto).

[16] Jonathan Swift, *Gulliver's Travels* (New York: Washington Square Press, 1939), p. 278.

[17] *The Autobiography of Martin Luther King, Jr.*, ed. Clayborne Carson (New York: Warner Brothers, 1998), p. 365.

[18] Unfortunately, I just couldn't find it again for this illustration.

[19] Goodreads.com, http://www.goodreads.com/quotes/show/3268.

[20] I'm indebted to an author I read decades ago for the thoughts in this and the following paragraph, both of which paragraphs may contain actual quotations from the particular source (now completely lost to me).

Chapter 13

Living in Crazy Times—and Staying Sober

"They came to Jesus and observed the man who had been demon-possessed sitting down, clothed and in his right mind" (Mark 5:15, NASB).

Novelette Sinclair was a shy 13-year-old girl when I knew her at the Westmount Adventist Church in Montreal in the late 1960s. But she grew up to be quite a young woman, excelling in school, "winning a scholarship to the University of Ottawa and earning a master's degree in linguistics in 1977."[1] Later she would teach French in Brussels and win a job as a translator at the United Nations in New York.[2]

But then one day she met David—as in David Koresh—and everything changed. Forsaking family and friends, she gave him all she had—her means, her body, and finally (together with more than 75 others) her life.[3]

David Koresh. Waco, Texas. The names have etched themselves into the psyche of people around the world as symbols of the madness and insanity of our times, taking their place in a kind of rogues' gallery of contemporary insanities that include such random names as Jim Jones, Ruby Ridge, Rwanda, Burundi, Bosnia, the New York World Trade Center, Oklahoma City, and September 11.

For months I'd struggled to wrap my head around it all, to define it, to give it a name. Finally, paralyzed by its sheer magnitude and complexity, I sat down one Sabbath morning, a blank notepad in front of me. One frustrating hour and two or three pages of random jottings later, a single compelling thought emerged that seemed to pull it all together for me: the seismic forces tearing society and the church apart toward the end of the past century and reaching into the present time have their roots in three basic factors—(1) an infantile gullibility, (2) a lunatic mentality, and (3) a twisted eschatology.

An Infantile Gullibility

You would think it could never happen again—not after Waco. Yet there it was. Thirty-nine bodies in an upscale neighborhood near San Diego, California, the remains of men and women who'd answered the call of Heaven's Gate cult leader, Marshall Applewhite, to shed their "containers" (their bodies) "and be transported after death by alien spacecraft riding shotgun in the sky for the Hale-Bopp comet."[4]

My first reaction was "Oh no, not again!" And the words of Washington *Post Magazine* writer Jeanne Marie Laskas, written several years earlier, came back to me. "How many times would we go around this circle?" she'd asked in the wake of the 1994 Solar Temple tragedy, in which more than 50 devotees of cult leader Luc Jouret's Order of the Solar Temple died in Switzerland and Canada. "It seems we're back here at the beginning, asking the same questions we were asking a year ago in Waco, Texas. The same questions we asked 16 years ago in Jonestown, Guyana. Apparently this cult story is going to keep repeating itself, as if there's some bad virus embedded in the human condition."[5]

Zeroing in on the amazing human gullibility even in our sophisticated times, Laskas told of her encounter with an Arizona-based group known as People Unlimited, or sometimes CBJ, after the initials of its three leaders: Charles Paul Brown, BernaDeane, and James Strole (known to their followers as "Chuck, Bernie, and Jim"). These three go around the world, she said, "teaching people how to be immortal." What we need, said the threesome, is "cellular awakening." "People who die are just stupid people, . . . people whose cells have been brainwashed by 'the death-oriented culture' into which we all were born. In order to become immortal, . . . all you have to do is to get your cells awakened by CBJ and then join with them in 'cellular intercourse.' "[6]

Someone from another planet might ask, "Who could possibly fall for such preposterous poppycock?" But after Marshall Applewhite and Heaven's Gate, we on this planet no longer wonder. Suckers for such absurdity could include college and university graduates just as easily as folk who've never heard a school bell ring. They could be people who have never so much as seen a telephone or whiz kids able to program sophisticated computers.

The people who fell for Koresh's claims were not stupid or uneducated. Novelette Sinclair, for one, was "a bright young woman who was clever enough to win university scholarships and capable enough to embark on an international career as a linguist, translator, and teacher."[7] Yet she fell for

Koresh's claim to be the new messiah, "the seventh and final angel who will bring about the end of the world." And with all the others, she swallowed it when he claimed "that by sleeping with him" his female followers would become "brides of Christ."[8]

Never should we underestimate the psychic grip of the cult leader. After attending a series of CBJ meetings, Laskas concluded "that people can have other people believing anything if the conditions are right. . . . People can be trained to believe in the ludicrous world according to Chuck-bernie-and-jim just as easily as they can the world according to Luc Jouret, David Koresh, Jim Jones, Charles Manson, Hitler. Anybody. People can be trained to sleepwalk their way into turning over their bank accounts, into drinking Kool-Aid laced with potassium cyanide, into shooting themselves in the head. Anything."[9]

And consider that after all the press coverage following the Heaven's Gate tragedy, one follower still went ahead with a copycat suicide weeks later; another follower was unsuccessful in the attempt; and the hotel in which the suicide occurred was flooded with calls from people wanting to book the same room, presumably for the same purpose.

People should know that when God calls us to serve Him, He does not ask us to disengage our intellects, put our minds in neutral, and enter a state of hapless gullibility. No, He calls us to love Him "with all [our] heart and with all [our] soul *and with all* [*our*] *mind*" (Matt. 22:37). God is vitally interested in the state of our minds:

"And they came to Jesus and observed the man who had been demon-possessed sitting down, clothed and in his right mind."

A Lunatic Mentality

Remember the March 1995 poison gas attack in a Tokyo subway by members of the Aum Shinrikyo cult that killed 12 people and injured more than 5,000? At his trial in a Tokyo courtroom two years later, the cult's 41-year-old guru, Shoko Asahara, gave his first public explanation of the incident, which turned out to be a classic in demented rambling. According to the New York *Times,* "Mr. Asahara said he had ordered his top aides to abort the planned gas attack two days before it occurred," but they disobeyed his orders. Instead, he said, they "persuaded him to go ahead with the attack." " 'In the end, it was me who was convinced by them,' he said. 'And that eventually led to my arrest.' "[10]

How frightening to think that such a scattered person was the head of an outfit with enough nerve gas and delivery equipment to kill millions of people! Often such groups are driven by a lunatic ideology based on conspiracy theories that have no basis in reality.

And their number is not diminishing. "What should be made of the fact," asks Liz Spayd, "that more than half of all Americans think flying saucers are real? That 49 percent of the public thinks the CIA was involved in the assassination of President Kennedy? Or that 9 percent of the public suspects, despite considerable evidence to the contrary, that the 1969 moon landing was a massive hoax?"[11] And it's well known that there are many Americans (and others) who believe that the U.S. government itself executed the September 11 attack for its own purposes.

Obsession with conspiracy theories is part of the lunacy of our times. Each weekend finds small groups of men and women in military-type fatigues training in some backwoods farm or forest in the United States against the day when, as they believe, federal government troops out to abolish individual rights will launch an attack on ordinary citizens. "Citizen militias, in what has emerged as one of the most vivid symbols of contemporary conspiracy [theories], insist that United Nations troops are circling around in black helicopters that they intend to use in a mass coup."[12]

Paranoia among such groups has only increased in recent years, and their number has grown significantly. In a March 7, 2012, *U.S. News/* MSNBC online article, Stephanie Schendel, citing the Southern Poverty Law Center (SPLC), reported that "the election of President Barack Obama in 2008 triggered an explosion in the number of militias and so-called patriot groups in the United States." "There were 149 militias and patriot groups when Obama took office," the report said, "compared to more than 1,200 today—an increase of 755 percent."[13]

Then there's the specter of international terrorism, one of the most frightening developments of our times, leaving many world leaders petrified over the prospect of evil people getting their hands on nuclear or other dangerous materials of mass destruction. Today American presidents, presumably the golden prize for terrorists, can take no chances as they travel within the United States or around the world. In his book *Are We Rome?* Cullen Murphy described the scene as former president George W. Bush arrived at Shannon Airport in the Irish Republic for an eight-hour official visit in the summer of 2008: "His two Air Force One jumbo jets were parked on the shiny tarmac, nose to nose. . . . A defensive perimeter of concertina wire surrounded [them]. Surface-to-air missiles backed it up.

The perimeter was manned by American forces in battle fatigues, flown in for the occasion—just one element of the president's U.S. security detail, a thousand strong. Other security personnel peered down from the rooftops of hangars and terminals, automatic weapons at the ready. Ringing the airport was a cordon of Scorpion tanks supplied by the Irish Republic."[14]

And there was more. U.S. Air Force cargo planes had brought in "helicopters, a dozen Secret Service SUVs, and the official presidential limousine . . . , its windows three inches thick and its doors so heavy with armor that gas-powered pistons must be used to help open them. Four U.S. naval vessels plied the Shannon River estuary nearby. Outside the airport the roads were jammed with Irish soldiers and police officers—6,000 in all."[15]

And there was more. But that's enough to make the point that we're living in a world that's crazier than it's ever been—and exceedingly more dangerous. In Murphy's words, "Governments can win only by defending everywhere; terrorists can win by succeeding anywhere."[16]

In the broader society—in the United States and many other Western countries—a kind of moral insanity has crept in. Even amid the rationalism of the seventeenth and eighteenth centuries, and well into the nineteenth and early twentieth centuries, the lines of morality and basic decency were pretty clearly drawn. Today, however, everything is blurred. And even conservative Christians (including Seventh-day Adventists) are showing increasing signs of confusion.

Western culture today is virtually under the control of the entertainment media, an entity that, in its multifaceted secular manifestations, contaminates just about everything it touches. Today most of the stuff coming from this giant molder of contemporary mores is nothing less than illustrated sermons from hell, exposing youngsters to hard-core portrayals of adult behavior in prime time and on the all-pervasive Internet. We're stealing the innocence of our children; we're corrupting them; we're ripening them before their time.

In a 1995 article commenting on daytime talk shows in America, Tom Shales pointed to the race "to be more outrageous, more salacious, more sensational." For a few minutes of fame, he said, people would divulge "their darkest secrets and their dirtiest laundry." And the multiplication of such programs has had the effect, he said, of inspiring producers "to aim not higher, but in fact lower; you can only outdo the other guy, it seems, by stooping further, by going for more sleaze and shouts and shocks." What we're watching, Shales said, is "the trashification of American culture."[17]

Today we have the technology to bring every species of vice directly into our homes merely by a click of the mouse beside our computers. And minors, generally far in advance of their parents and elders in computer literacy, are dabbling in hard-core materials in the privacy of their own rooms. If I were the devil out to confuse and destabilize modern society, I would do exactly what he's doing now. I would glorify gratuitous violence, glamorize illicit sex, and make it chic to be deviant. And I would make those who dare speak out against these developments look like benighted Victorian prudes, Neanderthals belonging to the unlit caves of a distant age.

We are facing, in all likelihood, the most unstable moral situation of any civilization in the history of human society. The entire moral ground is shifting under our feet. We're treading on quicksand.

The only solution for the present lunacy is Jesus. We must bring to Him our folly, our fears, our anger, our pride, our stupidity, our ignorance, our vulgarity, our immorality, our lunatic mentality. Only He can drive the "demons" out.

"*And they came to Jesus and observed the man who had been demon-possessed sitting down, clothed and in his right mind.*"

A Twisted Eschatology

Washington Post Magazine staff writer Peter Carlson went to Philadelphia back in 1994 to visit a certain Ted Daniels, editor/publisher of something called the "Millennium Prophecy Report." Daniels, a Ph.D. in folklore from the University of Pennsylvania, had been monitoring prophetic predictions across the United States in connection with the year 2000. From the back of a postcard with the picture of a flying saucer, Daniels read to Carlson the following prophecy:

"In A.D. 2001, starships from the Interplanetary Confederation [whatever that is] will land on earth carrying 33,000 Brothers! They're extraterrestrial teachers and scientists who will help us expand our understanding."[18]

Carlson's article, a brilliant summary of the tremendous hype in the run-up to the year 2000, cataloged the preoccupation of Americans with the coming millennium. Citing *Ancient Prophecies*, an NBC television special in the spring of 1994, Carlson noted the following confluence of predictions pointing toward the year 2000:

"The pyramids contain a coded calendar that shows the world ending on May 5, 2000. . . . Saint Malachy of Ireland predicted in the 1100s the names of all the popes until the end of time, and there are two popes to go. . . . Nostradamus saw disaster coming from the sky in 1999."

There's more: "The Blessed Virgin appeared at Fatima making a prediction that is so frightening that the pope is keeping it secret. . . . The book of Revelation portrays an apocalypse that may begin soon."

Predictions about geological and cosmic catastrophes abounded also: "Edgar Cayce, the famous 'sleeping prophet,' predicted that before 1998 the poles would shift and California would fall into the sea. . . . Paul Solomon, known as the 'second Cayce,' predicted that America would split right down the middle in the year 2000. . . . The ancient cabala says that a ball of fire will descend on man around the millennium."[19]

From our perspective today, we know the obvious outcome of all these prognostications. They failed, and life continues. But damage has been done to the integrity of the Bible, by associating it, as the NBC program did, with this catalog of hoity-toity predictions.

Nevertheless, the excitement and hysteria continues as society lurches from one fad to another—whether it be the *Left Behind* frenzy, the *Harry Potter* craze, the *Da Vinci Code* hype, the *Hunger Games* rage, or the recent 2012 apocalyptic scare. In regard to that last obsession, the movie thriller *2012* had raised its profile exponentially, with the eyes of millions around the world glued to December 21, 2012, as judgment day or Armageddon, the day when "a global cataclysm [will bring] an end to the world."[20] Even NASA had to set up a special Web site to answer the flood of questions it was receiving about the widely anticipated doomsday, now also shelved.[21]

Such hysteria can prove profoundly detrimental to prophetic preaching. Eventually, it could lead to prediction fatigue, millions shrugging the proverbial shoulder and saying: "Where is the promise of his coming?" (2 Peter 3:4, KJV).

Yet that very event is the ultimate expectation of the church. "If we lose this hope," as H.M.S. Richards, Sr., used to say, "we lose everything."

It's a precarious time for Seventh-day Adventists. None of us wants to come across as putting the coming of Christ off into the distant future. But however eager we are for the Lord to come, we ought never to resort to irresponsible speculation. For most of us, the recent end-of-the-world predictions by California radio evangelist Harold Camping are still fresh—his most notable prediction claiming that judgment day would arrive on May 21, 2011. Scoffers and skeptics had a field day with it, and jokes about the prediction stretched all around the world. The passing of the deadline left Camping "bewildered" and "mystified," according to reports. But, alas, it perhaps left doubters and skeptics emboldened in their resistance to God and religion.

Seventh-day Adventists have never officially set a date for the second coming.[22] But some Adventists in the recent past have dabbled in jubilee calculations, and others have read their own ideas into Ellen White's references to "6,000 years" as the reign of sin on earth. But to give any specifics for the *time* of the Second Advent—whether it be a particular month, year, decade, or generation—is to fall into the trap of time setting. And we must not.

The identity of that day is hidden in the inscrutable wisdom of God. But it will certainly happen. And when it does, God's people from all around the world will, like the ancient demoniac, fall at the feet of Jesus, our King—our infantile gullibility *gone,* our lunatic mentality *cured,* our twisted eschatology *corrected* in the marvelous light of His glorious presence.

---

[1] Andrew Phillips et al., in *Maclean's,* May 3, 1993, p. 20.

[2] *Ibid.*

[3] The Waco tragedy that took Sinclair's life began February 28, 1993, when four federal agents, among a larger group attempting to serve a warrant on David Koresh's Branch Davidian compound near Waco, Texas, were killed in a gunfire that erupted. Fifty days later (April 19), under heavy siege by the FBI, a fire broke out in the compound, resulting in the death of Koresh and more than 75 of his followers.

[4] *U.S. News and World Report,* Apr. 7, 1997, p. 26.

[5] Jeanne Marie Laskas, "Predators and Prayers," *Washington Post Magazine,* Nov. 6, 1994, p. 5.

[6] *Ibid.*

[7] *Maclean's,* p. 17.

[8] *Ibid.,* pp. 21, 22.

[9] Laskas, p. 5.

[10] "Cult Guru Accused . . . ," New York *Times,* Apr. 25, 1997, p. A-7.

[11] Liz Spayd, "Welcome to the State of Paranoia," Washington *Post,* July 23, 1995, p. C-1.

[12] *Ibid.,* p. C-2.

[13] Stephanie Schendel, "Election, Economy Spark Explosive Growth of Militias," *U.S. News,* http://usnews.msnbc.msn.com/_news/2012/03/07/10602763-election-economy-spark-explosive-growth-of-militias.

[14] Cullen Murphy, *Are We Rome?: The Fall of an Empire and the Fate of America* (Boston: Houghton Mifflin, 2007), pp. 3, 4.

[15] *Ibid.,* p. 4.

[16] *Ibid.,* p. 20.

[17] Tom Shales, "We're Mad as Hell at Daytime TV, Getting Sleazier by the Minute," Washington *Post,* Mar. 19, 1995, p. G-5.

[18] Peter Carlson, "The End," *Washington Post Magazine,* Jan. 1, 1995, p. 10.

[19] *Ibid.,* p. 13.

[20] "2012 Apocalypse: Is It Really Coming?" http://2012apocalypse.net/; http://www.imdb.com/title/tt1190080/.

[21] "Beyond 2012: Why the World Didn't End," Dec. 22, 2012, Frequently Asked Questions, NASA, http://www.nasa.gov/topics/earth/features/2012.html.

[22] Adventists freely acknowledge their connection to the time-setting Millerites. But once formed into a distinct denominational entity, Adventists as a church have never set a date for the Advent.

Chapter 14

Interpreting the Signs: Avoiding Hysteria and Staying Close to Scripture

Bob Schieffer, the CBS news anchor that day, came out with the unusual words, completely out of character for the *Evening News*. The reporter in the field had just finished a story on the massive earthquake in Pakistan and Kashmir (2005), with some 75,000 dead up to that point. In his distinctive Texan drawl, Schieffer said to his colleague in the field, "Tell me, recently we've been seeing all kinds of devastation and calamity and upheaval all around the world; what do you think is going on on the earth?"

The way he phrased the question caught my attention, and I wrote it down. "What do you think is going on on the earth?" Or to rephrase him, *What do these things mean? How should we interpret them?*

In September 2005 I listened to a fiery young Adventist preacher talking about the signs of the times, specifically in connection with Hurricanes Katrina, Rita, and other natural and human-made calamities that had either just occurred or had been predicted. As he waxed eloquent in his message, he asked his audience, "Have we ever seen anything like this before? These," he said, "are the most significant disasters in history!"

Continuing, he cited "two economic analysts" he'd heard on the news the previous evening. They'd indicated, he said, that Hurricanes Katrina and Rita "could potentially destroy . . . the economy" of the United States. The two economic analysts also said, according to him, "that by next week [which would have been about the end of September 2005], we could see gas prices rise to $6 a gallon!" (which, incidentally, did not happen). All of these things, he said with passion, show that "the world we're living in today is the end as we know it."

I found his statements particularly curious, having at the time just returned from the United Kingdom, where the price of gas was close to $9 a gallon. For this young preacher, Hurricanes Katrina and Rita, the crumbling of the American economy, and gas prices rising to $6 a gallon spelled "the end as we know it." When fellow Adventists say amen to such talk, I want with all my heart to join them. But something inside me wants to think first. I guess it comes from a concern for the long-term credibility of the church.

Like most Adventists, I'm paying attention to the events taking place in our time. The horrendous incident of December 26, 2004, for example, the day that massive tsunami killed more than a quarter million people in Asia in a single blow. One can hardly ignore events of such frightening magnitude.

But the question is What do they mean? How shall we interpret them? For horrible as they might be, they're nevertheless silent; they do not speak.

Which reminds me of the old legend about Moishe and the pope.

Legend With a Lesson

According to the tale, which comes in many versions, the pope about a century ago decreed that all Jews should leave Rome. But seeing the uproar in the Jewish population and wanting to appear conciliatory, he came up with a novel idea. He would have a debate with any member of the Jewish community they chose. If that person won the debate, then the Jews could stay, but if the pope won, the Jews would have to go. With all the educated, high-powered Jews reluctant to confront this Christian Goliath, the community eventually turned to an old janitor named Moishe.

However, feeling woefully inadequate to match the pope in verbal combat, Moishe suggested the debate should proceed in total silence, to which the pope, surprisingly, agreed.

As the eventful day arrived, Moishe and the pope sat down on opposite ends of a table and, for a full minute, stared at each other in motionless silence. At last, the pope raised his hand and showed three fingers. In response, Moishe raised one finger.

The pope then waved his hand in a circle around his head. Responding, Moishe vigorously pointed his finger to the ground where they sat.

Then the pope, bringing out a wafer (the Communion bread) and a glass of wine, set them on the table. In response, Moishe pulled out an apple and placed it down in front of him.

At this development the pope stood up and said, "I give up. This man is too good. The Jews can stay."

After the meeting, the cardinals gathered around the pope to learn what really happened. The pope said, "First, I held up three fingers to represent the Trinity; he responded by holding up one finger to remind me that there is still one God, common to both Christians and Jews. Then I waved my hand around my head to demonstrate that God was all around us; he responded by pointing his finger to the ground, showing that God was also right here with us. I pulled out the wine and the wafer to show that God absolves us of our sins; he, for his part, pulled out an apple to remind me of original sin. He had an answer for everything. What could I do?"

Meanwhile, the Jewish community had crowded around Moishe, amazed that this uneducated janitor could do what all their scholars believed was impossible. "What happened?" they asked him.

"Well," said Moishe, "first he raised three fingers to tell me that the Jews had three days to get out of Rome; I lifted one finger to tell him that *not one of us* was leaving. Then waving his hand around his head, he told me that this whole city would be cleared of Jews; I pointed my finger to the ground to let him know that we were staying right here."

"And then . . . and then?" asked one woman.

"I don't know," said Moishe. "He took out his lunch and I took out mine."

The lesson I take from the story is this: We might all be looking at the same events, the same signs, the same evidences. But these events, these signs, these evidences are all silent; they do not speak; they have no voice. And the interpretation we bring to them often arises from our own personal background or presuppositions.

That's why it's vital for us to go back every so often, take a seat at the feet of Jesus, and listen again—with more attentive, less prejudiced ears—to what He has to say as He speaks directly to the issue of the end of the world. And one of His most sustained treatments of this theme comes in Matthew 24. I will focus on only the first 14 verses, which effectively summarize, I think, the entire discourse.

Calm and Unhysterical

In response to His disciples' drooling admiration of the Temple, Jesus in verses 1 and 2 solemnly predicted the building's demise. Shocked, some approached Him privately, seeking clarification: "When will this happen, and what will be the sign of your coming and of the end of the age?" (verse 3).

Their question focused on two things: time and signs. Jesus would address both, but it's critical to notice what came first in His response. As if their concern about time and signs had failed to register, Jesus said, "Watch out that no one deceives you" (verse 4).

The matter of deception is critical in Jesus' response, and I return to it below. But for now, look at verses 6 to 8: "You will hear of wars and rumors of wars, but see to it that you are not alarmed. Such things must happen, but the end is still to come. Nation will rise against nation, and kingdom against kingdom. There will be famines and earthquakes in various places. All these are the beginning of birth pains."

What I notice here is the calmness of Jesus, the absence of hysteria. In the wake of calamity and disaster, the disciples should not expect the end to come the next day. Instead, Jesus outlined for them the scenario of an extended future. "Such things," He said, "must happen, but the end is still to come." ("But the end is not yet" [KJV].) In other words, we should not try to make a direct connection between military conflict or natural disasters and the Second Coming.

Take earthquakes, for example (see verse 7). A big one hit Pakistan in 2005, as mentioned above, killing between 75,000 and 79,000. Immediately following that disaster, while the media was full of reports on the event, one might have mounted the typical Adventist pulpit and solemnly proclaimed that it all showed the coming of Jesus to be "very, very soon." And the typical response from the congregation would have been a resounding "Amen!"

But here's what we'd find if we stopped long enough to take a look at history:

- A.D. 856: an earthquake strikes Damghan, Iran, killing 200,000 people. (That was more than 1,100 years ago!)
- August 9, 1138: an earthquake strikes Aleppo, Syria, leaving 230,000 dead.
- 1556—more than 456 years ago: an earthquake strikes Shaanxi, China, leaving 830,000 dead.

It's the kind of evidence a historian can throw at us when we base our case on the latest earthquake or other natural calamity to hit the news.

As Adventists, to mention another example, we've traditionally tended to link the Second Coming to war and economic crisis. During the First and Second World Wars, our evangelistic preaching was rife with predictions that this was it! (And from a human standpoint, and given certain presuppositions, it did look like it!) But the wars ended, and the Second Advent did not occur.

The Great Depression of the late 1920s/early 1930s saw millions out of work, multitudes homeless and hungry; it was an economic meltdown of major proportions. But the Great Depression did not trigger the Second Coming.

As the Gulf War was about to commence in 1991, with Saddam Hussein issuing dire warnings about "the mother of all battles," our prophetic juices stirred up again, some Adventists mounting pulpits and rushing into print with warnings about the Battle of Armageddon.

Today the frenzy continues. One Adventist worker a few years back claimed to possess secret intelligence, gleaned from some unnamed evangelical pastor, that the president of the United States (George W. Bush at the time) had given sealed orders to the entire armed forces of the country as to what to do when the next crisis broke—either through a terrorist attack or a financial collapse. The families of military personnel would have two hours to get out of the cities and head for the mountains or isolated towns. All major American cities would be sealed off, with no one allowed to enter or leave. According to the report the Adventist worker received, the American military already had in storage millions of casket liners—500,000 in the Atlanta, Georgia, area alone—presumably to dump the bodies of the millions who'd be killed.

Accordingly, the brother suggested, Adventists should also have a stash of food at the ready and be prepared to flee to the hills.

When we succumb to such hysteria, we degrade the value of prophecy and make religion a circuslike curiosity in the eyes of people who might otherwise be sympathetic listeners and even potential believers. Let's remember that our pious predictions of the nearness of the Coming based on the latest calamity do not influence the time of that event. If they did, then Jesus would have been here since the mid-nineteenth century, a time of unprecedented Advent expectation and fervor.

We need often to remind ourselves that we're talking here about the Sovereign God of the universe. He is not flustered by human whims; and in the words of Ellen G. White, His "purposes know no haste and no delay."[1]

So what was Jesus saying that day on the Mount of Olives? He was making the point that the age-old conflicts, which arise from human greed, arrogance, passion, and stupidity, will continue to play out on the stage of human history for an extended period: "Nation will rise against nation, and kingdom against kingdom" (verse 7). But such events would not trigger the Second Advent. He was drawing a picture of a planet groaning under the burden of human sin, a planet breaking down and steadily falling apart as that great day approaches. But these events, by themselves, do not pinpoint the time of the Second Coming.

What Should Concern Us Most

What should give us the greatest concern as we read Matthew 24 is not what Jesus said about wars, earthquakes, famines, and pestilences, but what He said about us! "Because of the increase of wickedness," He said in verse 12, "the love of most will grow cold." Everywhere we turn today—on city streets and billboards, in drugstores and supermarkets, on television and the Internet, in clubs and theaters—we are bombarded by sounds and images calculated to bring us down. The entire ground is shifting under our feet in a gigantic, spiritual earthquake, magnitude 8.9 on the moral Richter scale and increasing in intensity.

But even more alarming are Jesus' statements in verses 9 and 10. Here He speaks about His followers being persecuted, put to death, and "hated by all nations" (heavy stuff!). Then He says, "At that time many will turn away from the faith and will betray and hate each other."

Against the backdrop of those predictions, hear this from Ellen G. White: "As the storm approaches, a large class who have professed faith in the third angel's message, but have not been sanctified through obedience to the truth, abandon their position and join the ranks of the opposition. . . . Men of talent and pleasing address, who once rejoiced in the truth, employ their powers to deceive and mislead souls. They become the most bitter enemies of their former brethren."[2]

Then look at verse 11 of Matthew 24: "And many false prophets will appear and deceive many people."

Deep down we consider ourselves the smartest generation. But in our midst are some of the most gullible souls who've ever walked the planet. The spring of 2005 saw thousands of people making pilgrimages to an underpass in Chicago, where seeping sewage water had created a stain thought to resemble the virgin Mary.

If a sewage water stain could produce such a response, imagine what will happen when the entity Paul called "the lawless one" appears, using "all sorts of displays of power through signs and wonders" (2 Thess. 2:9)? Imagine what will happen if what Ellen White says in the following statement comes to pass exactly as she wrote it:

"As the crowning act in the great drama of deception, Satan himself will personate Christ. . . . In different parts of the earth, Satan will manifest himself among men as a majestic being of dazzling brightness," she says. "The glory that surrounds him is unsurpassed by anything that mortal eyes have yet beheld. The shout of triumph rings out upon the air 'Christ has come! Christ has come!'" Continuing, White says, "The people prostrate themselves in adoration before him, while he lifts up his hands and pronounces a blessing upon them. . . . He heals the diseases of the people, and then, in his assumed character of Christ, he claims to have changed the Sabbath to Sunday. . . . This is the strong, almost overmastering delusion"[3]

These are the things that should concern us most. Will we stand faithful in the face of the kind of pressure that certainly will accompany such hair-raising developments? Jesus said, "But the one who stands firm to the end will be saved" (Matt. 24:13).

The Pinnacle of the Passage

If we're looking for a sign that would signal the imminence of Jesus' coming, then the place to find it is Matthew 24:14: "And this gospel of the kingdom will be preached in the whole world as a testimony to all nations, and then the end will come."

It's not a flashy sign; it does not attract hysterical attention; it does not press panic buttons. But it's the only sign Jesus seemed to tie directly to His return.

We might be tempted to take perverse comfort in the apparently slow advance of the gospel and assume we could have our fling in the world, keep one eye out for the fulfillment of the gospel commission, and then jump back into shape at the eleventh hour. But that would be foolhardy. In the first place, the fulfillment of the preaching of the gospel in all the world is not something we can humanly measure. As humans we cannot know when this task will have been completed to the satisfaction of God's inscrutable wisdom. Nor can we have any idea of the multitude of agencies our omnipotent God has deployed to accomplish His work among the nations.

A second consideration on this point is the uncertainty of life. On the morning of September 11, 2001, more than 15,000 precious individuals made their way to their offices and appointments in the massive twin towers across from the Hudson River in New York City. No one even vaguely suspected anything but a normal day. But seconds past 8:46 a.m. all hell broke loose, and thousands were blown to shreds without a moment's warning!

Our only security is to anchor ourselves in God today, allowing the Great Commission to be fulfilled *in* us and *through* us.

And as regards the time of Jesus' coming, our attitude should be that of William Miller after the Great Disappointment of 1844: "I have fixed my mind upon another time," he said, "and here I mean to stand until God gives me more light—and that is Today, TODAY, and TODAY, until He comes, and I see Him for whom my soul yearns."[4]

---

[1] E. G. White, *The Desire of Ages*, p. 32.

[2] Ellen G. White, *The Great Controversy* (Mountain View, Calif.: Pacific Press Pub. Assn., 1911), p. 608.

[3] *Ibid.*, p. 624.

[4] William Miller letter, Nov. 10, 1844, in *The Midnight Cry*, Dec. 5, 1844, pp. 179, 180.

Chapter 15

Why Are We Still Here? A Question That Haunts Many Adventists Today

Some of you may remember the anxiety, the tension, the hype in the run-up to the year 2000—the fear that all our computer systems would collapse, and with them our entire infrastructure, with planes crashing and factories blowing up, etc. Frightening stuff!

So as the first day of that new year arrived, everyone breathed a sigh of relief—either out of gratitude that we'd survived or out of relief that the big hype about Y2K was gone.

That New Year's Day fell on a Sabbath, and following the service at my local church, two colleagues and I happened to meet in the middle of the sanctuary and fell into conversation. The discussion drifted to the second coming of Jesus, all three of us agreeing that a psychological sea change had just taken place. We had left the 1900s and had entered the 2000s.

And one of us asked the question How can we as Adventist Christians still maintain a sense of urgency about the Second Coming? After all, our pioneers thought the event was imminent way back in the middle of the nineteenth century (1844, to be exact)—some 155 years to the time of the new millennium! If Adventists of that generation (people such as Joseph Bates, J. N. Andrews, James and Ellen White) should rise from the dead today and discover that we're still here, they'd perhaps drop dead again from shock, never expecting the world would have lasted another 170 years!

So why are we still here? How would you finish the sentence "We are still here because . . ."?

It would be enlightening to tap into the responses of all 17 million Adventists around the world—enlightening and instructive. Because I suspect that many of the divisive theological issues that have vexed the Adventist Church in the recent past and up to the present derive directly or indirectly from the way we relate to that question. And our response, though often subliminal, determines whether we are happy, attractive, hopeful Adventists or disgruntled, critical, and morose; whether we are daily anchoring ourselves ever more deeply in Christ or struggling to showcase our own righteousness.

Facing the Question

In a narrow sense (that is to say, in the Adventist context), the question is a fair one, especially when raised against the background of statements by Ellen G. White as early as the mid-nineteenth century advocating the imminence of the Advent. Acknowledging in 1849 that "time has continued a few years longer than [we] expected," she nevertheless issued this sobering warning: "I saw that the time for Jesus to be in the most holy place was nearly finished and that time can last but a very little longer."[1]

"Time is almost finished," she wrote the next year, and new converts coming into the church "will have to learn in a few months" what had taken her and other old-timers years to master.[2] In 1856 she "was shown" that some in a group assembled for a conference in Battle Creek "will be alive and remain upon the earth to be translated at the coming of Jesus."[3]

If such statements (and there are others in that vein)[4] are to be taken at face value, the delay, from the human standpoint, at least, is not simply apparent but real. Something happened. Something went wrong. If we can put our finger on it, then we will have found at least a partial answer to the main question before us.

Ellen White's Own Position

As we might expect, the passage of time made it inevitable that Ellen G. White herself should confront the issue of a delay in the fulfillment of her own expectations and predictions. How did she handle it?

In one place she wrote as follows: "If all who had labored unitedly in the work of 1844 had received the third angel's message and proclaimed it in the power of the Holy Spirit, the Lord would have wrought mightily with their efforts. A flood of light would have been shed upon the world. Years ago the inhabitants of the earth would have been warned, the closing work would have been completed, and Christ would have come for the redemption of His people."[5]

Can anyone have any doubt as to what that statement gives as the fundamental reason God waits? Clearly, it is the lagging fulfillment of the gospel commission. As Scripture says, God does not want "anyone to perish, but everyone to come to repentance" (2 Peter 3:9).

Ellen White's statements addressing the delay almost invariably contain two elements: (1) a perishing world unwarned and (2) a lethargic remnant failing in its mission.

Around 1862, for example, she referred to a satanic "death stupor" resting on God's people while "all heaven is astir" over the proclamation of the final warning.[6] In 1883 she pointed to the "unbelief, the worldliness, unconsecration, and strife" among Adventist believers as responsible for their long sojourn in this world.[7] "Unbelief," she said in 1893, rests upon the church "like the pall of death," preventing it from "imparting the light to those who know not the precious truth."[8] While "multitudes" perish, she wrote around the turn of the century, "few of the professed followers of Christ are burdened for these souls."[9]

"Had the purpose of God been carried out by His people in giving to the world the message of mercy," she wrote in 1900, "Christ would, ere this, have come to the earth, and the saints would have received their welcome into the city of God."[10]

Her emphasis was the same in 1909, six years before her death: "If every watchman on the walls of Zion had given the trumpet a certain sound, the world might ere this have heard the message of warning. But the work is years behind."[11]

On the basis of this philosophy she could say, in reference to 2 Peter 3:12, that "by giving the gospel to the world it is in our power to hasten our Lord's return."[12]

No Linkage

I do not find in Ellen G. White's own accounts any attempt to link the delay of Christ's return to the idea of a perfect, sinless remnant. That linkage simply is not there. Her references to the spiritual state of God's people have the same tone as those to the world in general. God does not want His professed people to be lost any more than He wants the world to go down to ruin. This comes through clearly in the following statement, written in 1868: "The long night of gloom is trying; but the morning is deferred in mercy, because if the Master should come, so many would be found unready. God's unwillingness to have His people perish has been the reason for so long delay."[13]

As every Adventist knows, she holds up before us the highest spiritual and moral standards. "Higher than the highest human thought can reach is God's ideal for His children," she said. "Godliness—godlikeness—is the goal to be reached."[14] But she does not advocate that the time of Christ's return is somehow delayed by our failure to reach a prescribed standard of righteousness. She is very clear: the coming of the Lord "will not tarry past the time that the message is borne to all nations, tongues, and peoples."[15] That was her fundamental focus.

The "Character of Christ" Statement

A key statement that factors into Adventist discussions of what will usher in Christ's return is the following: "Christ is waiting with longing desire for the manifestation of Himself in His church. When the character of Christ shall be perfectly reproduced in His people, then He will come to claim them as His own."[16]

Fortunately, the statement does not appear in isolation. It comes with considerable context around it, a careful study of which will show that while it obviously has an inward-looking dimension, its fundamental focus is outward. "The character of Christ" here is equivalent to "the Spirit of unselfish love and labor for others," a concept that appears in a parallel thought right across the page and in the same context: "As you receive the Spirit of Christ—the Spirit of unselfish love and labor for others—you will grow and bring forth fruit. The graces of the Spirit will ripen in your character. Your faith will increase, your convictions deepen, your love be made perfect. More and more you will reflect the likeness of Christ in all that is pure, noble, and lovely."[17] Ellen White's burden throughout the chapter in question was that of *incarnational ministry, unselfish ministry*. Ministry patterned after that of Jesus. Read the chapter for yourself and see if this is not so.

When we speak like this, some think we're watering down the "straight testimony," that we're making light of the kind of deep spiritual preparation necessary to meet the Lord. But that is to misunderstand the awesome power of the kind of ministry envisioned here, as well as the strength of spiritual commitment and surrender from which it flows. Hear it in the words of Ellen G. White: "If we would humble ourselves before God, and be kind and courteous and tenderhearted and pitiful, there would be one hundred conversions to the truth where now there is only one. But . . . we carry around with us a bundle of self. . . . It is our privilege to lay this burden at the feet of Christ and in its place take the character and similitude of Christ."[18]

The emphasis in the judgment will be on that kind of ministry. The whole world will be divided into just two groups. Those whom the King commends will have demonstrated in their lives the practical outworking of the character (or spirit) of Christ. Says the King to them: "I was hungry and you gave me something to eat, I was thirsty and you gave me something to drink, I was a stranger and you invited me in, I needed clothes and you clothed me, I was sick and you looked after me, I was in prison and you came to visit me" (Matt. 25:35, 36).

This is the kind of ministry that will commend the gospel to rich and poor and speed its message across racial, cultural, and national barriers. The complete opposite of navel-gazing, it will arrest the attention of a cynical generation. That's what Ellen White is talking about in her "character of Christ" statement.[19]

From Another Perspective

Let's return to the basic question as to why we're still here. We have conceded that in a narrow sense it is a fair and valid query. But in the wider context it opens up the issue as one that confronts the Christian church as a whole, and not just Seventh-day Adventists. For clearly the New Testament writers spoke about the Advent with an urgency equal to that of Ellen White. And if anything, they were (in a manner of speaking) further from the mark than she was, for they wrote earlier.

But whether in the case of Paul or Peter or Ellen White, the emphasis on the nearness of the Second Advent was always given for a practical purpose, for the sake of the way we live and witness in the world, never for the sake of time, as such.

When it came to the raw question of time, Paul sought to keep in check overly enthusiastic believers, some of whom had even claimed that the Coming had already taken place. "That day will not come," Paul said, "until . . . the man of lawlessness is revealed" (2 Thess. 2:3). In a similar manner White, around 1868, sought to calm things a bit when she observed that "the Lord intimates a delay before the morning finally dawns."[20]

So while the question as to why we're still here is a reasonable one in view of our history, it will weigh us down spiritually and emotionally if we do not at some point break free of that history and see the crass presumptuousness of it. This is what Jesus tried to get across to His disciples when on the eve of the Ascension He told them plainly, "It is not for you to know the times or dates the Father has set by his own authority" (Acts 1:7).

It's not really your business, Jesus was gently saying to them. And there is a sense in which the same is true for us.[21]

As Seventh-day Adventists we need to recapture the concept of God's sovereignty. We need ever to keep in mind that from God's standpoint there is really no delay and we shouldn't get uptight about it. "Like the stars in the vast circuit of their appointed path, God's purposes know no haste and no delay." In heaven's council, said Ellen White, speaking about the First Advent, "the hour for the coming of Christ had been determined. When the great clock of time pointed to that hour, Jesus was born in Bethlehem."[22]

And thus it will be with the Second Advent. "The apparent tarrying is not so in reality, for at the appointed time our Lord will come."[23]

So why are we still here? In a sense, that question has effectively been answered in the foregoing discussion: the job is not yet done. A companion question, however—and perhaps the one we really want to ask—is, How long before we leave? To that, only God knows the answer. And really, only God needs to know.

---

[1] Ellen G. White, *Early Writings* (Mountain View, Calif.: Pacific Press Pub. Assn., 1882), p. 58.

[2] *Ibid.*, p. 67.

[3] Ellen G. White, *Testimonies for the Church* (Mountain View, Calif.: Pacific Press Pub. Assn., 1948), vol. 1, pp. 131, 132.

[4] For a convenient summary and assessment of similar statements, see Ralph Neall, *How Long, O Lord?* (Hagerstown, Md.: Review and Herald Pub. Assn., 1988), pp. 47-50.

[5] E. G. White, *Testimonies*, vol. 8, p. 116.

[6] *Ibid.*, vol. 1, pp. 260, 261.

[7] Ellen G. White, *Evangelism* (Washington, D.C.: Review and Herald Pub. Assn., 1946), p. 696.

[8] Ellen G. White, *Christian Service* (Washington, D.C.: Review and Herald Pub. Assn., 1925), p. 37.

[9] E. G. White, *Christ's Object Lessons*, p. 303.

[10] E. G. White, *Testimonies*, vol. 6, p. 450.

[11] *Ibid.*, vol. 9, p. 29.

[12] E. G. White, *The Desire of Ages*, p. 633.

[13] E. G. White, *Testimonies*, vol. 2, p. 194: cf. E. G. White, *Evangelism*, p. 694.

[14] Ellen G. White, *Messages to Young People* (Nashville: Southern Pub. Assn., 1930), p. 40.

[15] E. G. White, *Evangelism*, p. 697.

[16] E. G. White, *Christ's Object Lessons*, p. 69.

[17] *Ibid.*, p. 68.

[18] E. G. White, *Testimonies*, vol. 9, pp. 189, 190.

[19] For a more focused study of the statement, see Roy Adams, "What Did She Mean?" *Adventist Review*, Sept. 3, 1992, p. 4.

[20] E. G. White, *Testimonies*, vol. 2, p. 192.

[21] For a similar emphasis, see Arnold Wallenkampf, *The Apparent Delay* (Hagerstown, Md.: Review and Herald Pub. Assn., 1994), pp. 49-54.

[22] E. G. White, *The Desire of Ages*, p. 32.

[23] E. G. White, *Manuscript Releases* (Silver Spring, Md.: Ellen G. White Estate, 1990), vol. 10, p. 270.

Chapter 16

On Borrowed Time: An Issue for Both Nations and Individuals

Sometimes I try to imagine how the Millerites felt in 1844. On July 22, for example, believing that Jesus would return in exactly three months! Or on October 15, seven days! Or on October 22—*today! Jesus is coming back today! Any minute now, the heavens will split asunder, and we shall see the face of God!*

But as the clock tolled 12:00 midnight, it all began to sink in: *Jesus isn't coming back today.*

And what they—and we—would discover was that Jesus wasn't coming back the next day either, nor the next week, nor the next month, nor the next year, nor the next decade, nor the next century! And here we are today, more than 169 years later, still on this planet.

In this chapter I want to share how I come to terms with the problem of what some refer to as "the delay."

I do just two things.

First, I grapple with the question of *veracity*. In other words, regardless of the *when* of the event, I try to settle in my own mind the matter of its *certainty*, its *integrity*. I do this by considering the credibility of the Person who made the promise in the first place. I picture Jesus sitting in the upper room of a house in Jerusalem, addressing a worried and apprehensive group of followers. And I hear Him calmly speak those critical words found in John 14:3: "And if I go and prepare a place for you, I will come back and take you to be with me."

And I believe Him!

If for no one else, that statement I just made is significant for *me*, knowing myself to be among the most skeptical souls on the planet—skeptical and perhaps more than a tad cynical. But when I consider the fact that Jesus was not a figment of the imagination—that He was an actual, undisputed historical figure; that He was crucified; that He rose from the dead, as attested to in the unaffected telling of the Gospel writers; and that the influence of His life and work is more than substantiated in the life of His followers and in human culture for two millennia—I find His promise to return utterly credible and convincing.

And I strengthen that belief by comparing the promise of the Second Advent with that of the First. The promise of the First Advent was given back in the Garden of Eden, when God said, "I will put enmity between you and the woman, and between your offspring and hers; he will crush your head, and you will strike his heel" (Gen. 3:15). Almost universally, theologians and biblical scholars recognize that statement as messianic, as a promise, in other words, of the coming of the Redeemer, a forecast of the first advent of Jesus.

But the world was to wait thousands of years for its fulfillment. Sages and prophets peered into the shadowy distance for it; and thousands of mothers in Israel, beginning with Eve, each hoped she'd be the one to nestle the world's Redeemer in her bosom. But they were disappointed again and again, generation after generation.

But as God's great cosmic clock struck the prescribed hour, the angel Gabriel was dispatched from the presence of God to a humble peasant girl in the little ghost of a town called Nazareth. "You will conceive," the angel said, "and give birth to a son, and you are to call him Jesus" (Luke 1:31). "When the fullness of the time had come, God sent His Son" (Gal. 4:4, NKJV). He was born in Bethlehem. And that holy night, angels sang to wondering shepherds: "Today in the town of David a Savior has been born to you; he is the Messiah, the Lord" (Luke 2:11).

The promise of the First Advent was delayed, so to speak. The world waited millennia for its fulfillment. But it did not fail. And so it will be with the second coming of Jesus.

When I'm tempted to become antsy over the passage of time, I think of Abraham, who, after receiving the promise of a son, waited some 25 years for its fulfillment, with his age fast approaching the century mark. We blame Sarah for taking matters into her own hands, but not without some understanding of her long-past-menopause plight.

Waiting on God should become a normal attitude for His followers. Think of the Israelite sojourn in Egypt—some 400 years long! Were we in their place and were 2014 to be the year of our liberation, we'd have been waiting since 1614! The celestial wheels do not always spin at a rate that satisfies our human frenzy or even what we might consider our reasonable expectations.

But those wheels *do* spin! And given God's track record, they will again "in the fullness of time."

The second thing I do in coming to grips with the issue of the apparent delay of the Advent is to wrestle with the reality of what's been called "borrowed time," both on *the personal level* and on a *global scale*.

An instructive scriptural example of the concept of borrowed time on the personal level is the case of Hezekiah, recorded in 2 Kings 20. In the midst of a prosperous reign, the 39-year-old monarch was suddenly stricken with a fatal disease, and the prophet Isaiah arrived at his home, not to pray for his healing, but to announce his death: "Put your house in order, because you are going to die; you will not recover" (verse 1).

The outlook for Hezekiah was as bleak as could be. With all his little remaining strength, he managed to turn away from his servants and bodyguards. And with his face toward the wall in privacy, he prayed to the One who had always been his refuge and strength, a very present help in trouble. He prayed and he wept.

God's answer came swiftly. "Before Isaiah had left the middle court, the word of the Lord came to him: 'Go back and tell Hezekiah, . . . "I have heard your prayer and seen your tears; I will heal you. . . . I will add fifteen years to your life" ' " (verses 4-6).

Fifteen years of borrowed time!

Might we also, as individuals, be living on borrowed time? Could it be that God's merciful providence has extended our time also? Many of us, old and young, can look back at close calls, times when we might have died, when we might have been killed. But we were spared.

My family and I were on our way from Orlando, Florida, to Manila, Philippines, the last day of December 1980, with a first stop in Atlanta, Georgia. Fifteen minutes after taking off from Atlanta, we ran into problems. "Ladies and gentlemen," the captain's voice sounded over the PA system, "we're experiencing some difficulties."

Not turbulence. "Difficulties"!

Airline crews are trained to use words that would not alarm passengers unduly. So when the captain spoke the word "difficulties," a relatively strong term, many passengers understood the situation was not to be classified as run-of-the-mill.

"Our landing gear appears to be stuck in the down position," he said.

That was, of course, better than being stuck in the up position, but unless the gear was stuck all the way down, our predicament could still be just as precarious. Stuck only partway down, they'd almost certainly collapse on landing and send the airplane sliding on its belly down the runway at 150 miles per hour. Not pretty. "We will have to return to Atlanta," the captain continued, "but first we must fly over the control tower and have them verify the position of the landing gear for us."

After what seemed an eternity, his voice came back, this time informing us that the plane was too heavy to attempt an immediate landing. Twenty thousand pounds of fuel must be dumped before we could put down. From where my family sat we could look out the window and see streams of fuel being pushed out into the air—not a very comforting feeling, you can be sure.

Everyone recognized we were in serious peril. Passengers looked at one another, each one groping for some little assurance in the other's face. Before takeoff, passengers—especially frequent fliers—gaze absentmindedly as the flight crew demonstrate the safety features of the aircraft. But in the present predicament I watched as a couple sitting diagonally across from us actually pulled out the safety information brochure from the seat pocket and began reading it. Some people, including yours truly, were visibly praying.

I said to my wife, Celia, "In the event of anything, take Dwayne and make for that exit over there. I will take Kim and attempt to reach that other one." (Our kids were 4 and 2 at the time.) It was an exceedingly frightening experience, a very close call.

No prophet came. No voice sounded the death knell in our ears that day. But we knew as we landed amid the fire engines that December morning that the God of Hezekiah had heard our prayers and in mercy had extended our lives for a little while longer.

Many reading these lines, I'm sure, can relate even more harrowing situations *they* have faced.

When we understand we're living on borrowed time and that God is extending the same grace to others everywhere, then we begin to grasp an essential reason for the apparent delay of the Advent. The great God of the universe does not bow to human pressure in order to "save face." God will not hurry and come down so as to save our chart makers and time setters from embarrassment. He is not that kind of God.

No, God will do whatever God must do to ensure the greatest good to the greatest possible number. For He is not willing that *any* should perish but that *all* should come to repentance (see 2 Peter 3:9).

That's the kind of God we have.

And how about borrowed time on a global scale? It's clear from the prophetic writings of the Bible that humanity has come far down the stream of time to what many have called the final days. The prophecy of Daniel 2, for example, a good portion of which the prophet interpreted right in the text itself, places the world—for centuries now—down into the very toes of the image, the time when God is to set up His everlasting kingdom (see verses 41-44).

The prophecy of Revelation 6, dealing with the opening of the seals of that book of destiny in the hand of God, takes us (as Adventists have interpreted it) from about A.D. 31 clear down to the end. As the sixth seal opens, there is, the text says, "a great earthquake. The sun turned black . . . , the whole moon turned blood red, and the stars in the sky fell to earth" (verses 12-14)—all these referring to events now in the distant past. And what's significant here is that the next cataclysmic development the passage mentions is that of the second coming of Jesus in the open skies (verses 13, 14).

This means that we're living now between verses 13 and 14 of Revelation 6—in a "holding pattern" now, so to speak, for more than 180 years.

Why? Because, I think, of the incredible patience and mercy of the Almighty; for in the next event following the falling of the stars, all heaven breaks loose, with the inhabitants of the earth pleading with the rocks and mountains to shelter them from the wrath of God (see verses 14-17).

Considering the enormity of these impending events, God holds back, which, I think, is the meaning of Revelation 7:1-3. The passage speaks of a moment when the time of the world is up and the angels of judgment are ready to carry out the "strange act" of God (see Isa. 28:21, KJV). But, as in the case of Hezekiah on the personal level, there is a respite, an extension of time, a postponement of probation's close on the cosmic level. An angel emerges from the heavenly sanctuary with a call to the judgment angels to hold their fire "until we put a seal on the foreheads of the servants of our God" (Rev. 7:3).

I think I've seen many instances in our times that seem to indicate the presence of supernatural agencies holding back the winds of global calamity. Consider, for example, the following apparently minor sparks that ignited huge conflagrations, compared to the major incidents today that do not as much as light a fire.

On Sunday, June 28, 1914, a gunman killed Archduke Franz Ferdinand (heir to the throne of Austria-Hungary) and his wife, Sophie, as they rode through the streets of Sarajevo, capital of the then Austrian province of

Bosnia. That single incident, which today might occupy not much more than two news cycles, ignited the massive conflagration of World War I, leaving between 9 million and 15 million people dead.[1] Likewise, World War II, which killed an estimated 55 million around the world, was triggered by a single event: Hitler's 1939 invasion of Poland.

So what I find intriguing is that a thousand skirmishes around the globe since World War II, now more than 67 years in the past, have not precipitated a third global conflict. We can mention the frightening days of the Korean War; the bloody years of the Vietnam War; the tense decades of the cold war, with the Soviet invasion of Hungary and Czechoslovakia. None of these succeeded in igniting global hostilities.

The reason for that seems clear. When one considers the casualties of World War II, the first war in which a nuclear device was used—55 million dead—then one has only to imagine the unspeakable nightmare that would result from a third worldwide conflict, which would likely involve thermo-nuclear weapons and other frightening devices of mass destruction. It would be an unprecedented global catastrophe that would obliterate literally hundreds of millions, not to mention leave the planet totally uninhabitable. That's why Revelation 7:1-3 draws a picture of supernatural forces holding back the winds of judgment and catastrophe.

The hair-raising confrontation between the United States and the (then) Soviet Union in the Cuban missile crisis of 1962 was a clear example of this divine restraint, I think. In his book *Thirteen Days*[2] Robert Kennedy, brother of former president John F. Kennedy, chronicled the events of that critical period, supplying the reader with intriguing behind-the-scenes information on the showdown. The following paragraphs are based on details in Kennedy's book.

The United States intelligence community had detected a huge missile buildup in Cuba, with photos indicating that the weapons were being directed at certain key American cities. The estimate was that within a few minutes of their firing, 80 million Americans would be dead.

That was the information that led to the 13-day crisis, beginning Tuesday, October 16. That day, a specially selected group of top administration officials began a concentrated focus on the developing problem. Working virtually around the clock, the group managed to come up with two recommendations for the president by late Friday of that first week. One called for a rocket attack on Cuba, an option all the Joint Chiefs of Staff supported. The other called for a military blockade of the island, an option Robert Kennedy, Robert McNamara, and a few others supported.

On Saturday morning Kennedy called the president at the Blackstone Hotel in Chicago and told him they were ready with the report. Canceling all his remaining appointments, the president returned to Washington immediately.

With *Air Force One* still in the air, the Armed Forces of the United States were placed on full alert. Four tactical air squadrons were put at readiness for an air attack on Cuba at a moment's notice, if ordered by the president. Troops were moved into Florida, and the Navy deployed 180 ships into the Caribbean. The B-52 bomber force was ordered into the air, fully loaded with nuclear weapons. As one came down to land, another immediately took its place in the air.

Few of us ordinary folk really knew how close we came to the brink. Fortunately, the president rejected the recommendation of the Joint Chiefs, opting instead for a military blockade.

The peak of the crisis came Wednesday of the following week, the ninth day. At 10:00 that morning, Secretary McNamara announced that two Russian ships were within just a few miles of the quarantine barrier. A few minutes later an ominous Navy report indicated that a Russian nuclear submarine had moved into position between the two ships. People around the world sat transfixed in front of radios and television sets.

Twenty-five anxious minutes later, at 10:25 that Wednesday morning, a messenger brought in a note to the president. It read, "Mr. President, we have a preliminary report . . . that some of the Russian ships have stopped dead in the water."[3]

As one who was intimately familiar with all of the relevant information, Robert Kennedy described the crisis as an event that "brought the world to the abyss of nuclear destruction and the end of mankind."[4] And in secret tapes recorded just before his death, Soviet president Nikita Khrushchev described the crisis as one that "placed the planet on the brink of extinction."[5] That's how close we came!

British prime minister Harold Macmillan made the following statement in a foreword to Kennedy's book: "There are many questions which still remain unanswered. Why did the Russians risk so much? What was their ultimate purpose? Why did they withdraw?"[6]

As students of prophecy, we have special intelligence on Macmillan's final question, Why did they withdraw? It comes from the picture we find in Revelation 7:1-3, mentioned above. An angel emerges from the open door of the heavenly sanctuary, the nerve center of our salvation, with a mighty cry to hold back the developing catastrophe for just a little longer, in mercy to humanity, until the servants of God are sealed in their foreheads. Ellen G. White in one place described the sealing as "a settling into the truth, both intellectually and spiritually, so [we] cannot be moved."[7]

That, I believe, is the silent, critical work going on right now in the hearts of men and women around the world. God will do all that He can do to save the largest number possible.

Nevertheless, God "has set a day when he will judge the world with justice" (Acts 17:31). No human being is privy to His timing. But we may have the assurance, God's love being what it is, that into His great cosmic "computer" He has entered all the incredibly complicated variables of every human life on earth and determined the optimum moment of Christ's second advent.

When that hour strikes, Jesus will come.

"It may be at morn, when the day is awaking,
When sunlight through darkness and shadow is breaking,
That Jesus will come in the fullness of glory
To receive from the world His own.

It may be at midday, it may be at twilight,
It may be, perchance, that the blackness of midnight
Will burst into light in the blaze of His glory,
When Jesus receives His own.

O Lord Jesus, how long, how long
Ere we shout the glad song?
Christ returneth, Hallelujah! hallelujah! Amen."[8]

---

[1] Sources vary regarding the estimated death toll of World War I.

[2] Robert F. Kennedy, *Thirteen Days: A Memoir of the Cuban Missile Crisis* (New York: W. W. Norton and Co., 1969).

[3] *Ibid.*, p. 71.

[4] *Ibid.*, p. 23.

[5] Associated Press, "Khrushchev Tape Says Castro Wanted War," Sept. 24, 1990, times union.com, http://alb.merlinone.net/mweb/wmsql.wm.request?oneimage&imageid=5545965

[6] Kennedy, pp. 18, 19.

[7] *The Seventh-day Adventist Bible Commentary,* Ellen G. White Comments, vol. 4, p. 1161.

[8] *The Seventh-day Adventist Hymnal*, no. 207.

Chapter 17

"But as for Me": Making a Difference in an Age of Idolatry

Now fear the Lord and serve him with all faithfulness. Throw away the gods your ancestors worshiped beyond the Euphrates River and in Egypt, and serve the Lord. But if serving the Lord seems undesirable to you, then choose for yourselves this day whom you will serve. . . . But as for me and my household, we will serve the Lord" (Joshua 24:14, 15).

In the spring of 2005 I came out with a book on Joshua entitled *Crossing Jordan: Joshua, Holy War, and God's Unfailing Promises,*[1] touching on some of the most critical issues facing both church and society today. Ever since that time, I've wanted to write something on the topic of this chapter, which began to impress itself upon me only after I'd written the book. But each time I approached the subject, the question would somehow come to me, Are you good enough to tackle it?

But most of us never come to the place where we feel "good enough." So I'm presenting this chapter with the understanding that I'm "preaching" to myself first.

I divide the topic into three ordinary, unembellished headings: (1) "Confronting the Subversive Power of Idolatry"; (2) "Making a Difference"; and (3) "Every Tub on Its Own Bottom."

Confronting the Subversive Power of Idolatry

One part of the Jacob-Laban story (see Gen. 31) has always intrigued me. Laban and his fighting men, armed to the teeth, overtake the fleeing Jacob and his comparatively unarmed, slow-moving party. The intention is to capture them and inflict the appropriate punishment for skipping town without notice. But during the previous night God warns Laban in a dream not to touch his fleeing nephew. And so all of Laban's fighting men, their nervous fingers on the triggers of their weapons (so to speak), are constrained to hold their fire.

Laban is angry that Jacob is absconding with his daughters, his grandchildren, and so much wealth. But he is absolutely beside himself for another reason: his household gods have been stolen. And he demands that Jacob return them.

For his part, Jacob is absolutely scandalized by this monstrous accusation. "Go through all my things," he says to Laban, "and kill the person with whom you find them."

The search begins and eventually reaches Rachel's tent. "Don't be angry, Dad, that I cannot stand up in your presence," Rachel says. "The condition of women is upon me." ("I'm having my period.") And she knows that no Eastern male would fool with that!

But what Laban does not know and Jacob does not realize is that *Rachel is actually sitting on her father's gods!*

And what has intrigued me is that that's the kind of god we like—gods we can sit on! It's absolutely incredible with what tenacity these useless gods can cling to our souls. Hundreds of years later—in Joshua's time—we would find the descendants of Jacob, people who had received all kinds of evidence of the power of the living God, still in cahoots with these utterly useless idols.

Hence, Joshua's appeal in Joshua 24:14; he says (I paraphrase him): "Throw these gods out!"

I find it utterly extraordinary that there should be the need for such an appeal at this juncture in the experience of Israel. To study even only briefly this period of Israel's history is to find yourself captured by the sheer magnitude of the events they'd witnessed, as summarized in Joshua 24 itself.

Hundreds of thousands (if not millions) of people arrive at the Red Sea in their flight from bondage with all their children, their household baggage, their animals and supplies—picture it. And here lying in their way is this massive body of water called the Red Sea. (We talk about it casually today because we know the outcome; *they* didn't!) Behind them is the Egyptian army in hot pursuit, armed to the teeth.

In that impossible extremity, God says to them, "Move forward!" And suddenly the sea opens up before them, and they walk through on solid ground!

Imagine Adventists facing this kind of crisis in the state of Maryland, where I live: They're being hunted down by their enemies. From our various localities, we assemble in the state capital of Annapolis along the shore of the Chesapeake Bay. Our pursuers, meanwhile, are approaching from three directions: north, west, and south. With the bay blocking our flight to the east, we're pinned down. But imagine that just when our enemies think we're hopelessly trapped, the waters of the Chesapeake open up in front of us and we escape on dry ground to the other side, while our enemies are overcome by the returning waters.

Can you imagine the sensation, the international wall-to-wall media coverage of the event? Would Adventists in Maryland—indeed, Adventists throughout the country—ever forget the astonishing event? ever stop talking about it? ever need to be admonished by another preacher about the need to be faithful to God?

That's what happened to Israel, except that it was several times more spectacular.

They come to Sinai and feel the very ground shake under their feet; they see the entire mountain covered in smoke and blazing fire; and they actually hear with their own ears the voice of the living God thundering down from the inferno. Would they ever forget that? Would *gods you can sit on* ever have a chance with them again?

They arrive at the Jordan. It's harvesttime and the river, at flood level, overflows all its banks—dangerous stuff. But they watch as the priests bearing the sacred ark of the covenant step forward; and before their very eyes the swollen river divides, with the water on their left draining down to the Dead Sea, while the water on their right, the Bible says, stands up in a heap!

Have you ever seen a thing like that? Water piled up in a heap! But it did then, held back by the awesome power of the living God. Could they ever again give allegiance to anything that competes with a God like that?

They come to Jericho and walk around the city seven days, as God commanded. And at the end of their seventh encirclement on the seventh day, as they shout in thunderous unison, invisible hands shake the walls of that impregnable fortress and brings them down. A few days later they hear Joshua command the sun itself to stand still in the heavens, and it obeys him. I mean, that's mind-blowing stuff!

Who would think a group of people who'd seen such eye-bulging wonders would ever need to be scolded about fake gods hidden in their closets and under their beds? But such is the grotesque perversity of the human heart. And such is the mesmerizing power of idolatry.

So as he approaches the end of his life, and in one of the most powerful challenges to loyalty and faithfulness in the entire Bible, Joshua calls on Israel in the name of God to abandon the useless gods of Mesopotamia and Egypt: "Choose for yourselves this day whom you will serve. . . . But as for me and my household, we will serve the Lord" (Joshua 24:15).

Making a Difference

Joshua had the gumption to confront idolatry in his time, bucking its subversive power. And he made a difference—a huge difference—as we find in verse 31: "Israel served the Lord throughout the lifetime of Joshua and of the elders who outlived him and who had experienced everything the Lord had done for Israel."

We too must confront the subversive power of idolatry in our own times and, by the grace of God, *make a difference.*

"Idolatry in our times?" I can hear someone say. "Please, get real! We've gone past that now. We don't dabble anymore in the infantile notion of idols and fake gods. Our modern sophistication has weaned us from such juvenile practices. *That's so yesterday!*"

Really?

In an eye-opening piece in the *USA Today* online edition back in February 2005, writer Maria Puente provided a graphic summary of our current preoccupation with celebrity and glamour, the idols of contemporary culture.[2] She mentioned the case of salesman Wade Jones of Charlotte, North Carolina. Jones said that in 1977, on his thirteenth birthday, he attended an Elvis Presley concert. And as soon as the program ended, he rushed up to the stage and grabbed the cup Elvis had been drinking from as he performed. He took it home (with its leftover water), secured it in plastic wrap, placed it in his freezer, and kept it there for more than 27 years. Eventually Jones sold those three tablespoons of water on eBay for $455. (And you think we're really more sophisticated today than the ancients? Four hundred fifty-five bucks for three tablespoons of frozen water from Elvis Presley's cup!)

Puente reported that collectors have vied for a cough drop Arnold Schwarzenegger had spit out; they've gone after Bryan Adams' dirty socks; they've competed for chewing gum said to have been discarded by Britney Spears. (Asking $99 for the piece of gum, the seller sweetened the offer by mentioning that the gum "still has saliva on it"!)

Justin Timberlake, said Puente, was eating breakfast at a New York radio station, where he'd appeared for an appointment, and when he finished, he left part of his French toast at the table. Someone picked it up and later sold it on eBay for $3,100.

Idols have not gone out of fashion; they've only changed names and shapes. Ours is an absolutely starstruck generation. The entertainment and other media personalities of our times command the allegiance, the attention, and, yes, the worship of untold millions around the world. And there's much anecdotal evidence *of their creeping influence within the Adventist Church, resulting in all kinds of subtle shifts in standards, in morals, and in spiritual fervor.*

The outlook is truly daunting. And sometimes leaders, struggling to keep their own heads above water, feel like dwarfs in the face of the influence wielded by these bigger-than-life superstars, bearing down on this generation like giant, morality-busting steamrollers.

But we all can make a difference—whether we're poor or rich, educated or not, and regardless of our abilities or disabilities. For my part, I'm confident this chapter (and this book), for example, will make a difference in some life somewhere, perhaps in ways that will forever remain unknown to me. The faculty and staff throughout my educational career have left lasting influences on my life that many of them will never know. One in particular whom I remember at this moment will certainly never have imagined that his contribution that morning in college worship decades ago had left an indelible impression on me.

It was the first chapel of the semester, and Mr. Clayton Enriques, a member of the faculty, stood before the student body and sang the following words from the depth of his soul and in a manner that has embedded itself in my consciousness forever. I was hearing the piece for the first time, and I have not heard it since; but its melody and message have stayed with me all these years:

"My life goes on, some days are good, some ill
O Father, let Thy loving presence fill
Both day and night; O hold me so I cannot fall,
For thou art Life and Strength, and my All in All.
Hold Thou my hand, dear Lord, hold Thou my hand;
I do not ask to see, nor understand;
Only that Thou wilt be constantly near to me,
Holding my hand, dear Lord,
Holding my hand."

I cannot tell you the number of times I've sung those precious words to myself since that day decades ago, drawing from them both courage and inspiration. I don't know whether Mr. Enriques is still alive or is deceased, but I would love to meet him in the kingdom and let him know the difference he made in my life through the simple rendition of that song, and the down-to-earth humility in his demeanor as he did so.

And you and I can make a difference too, in some person's life, if we simply let Christ shine through us, the surrounding darkness notwithstanding.

Every Tub on Its Own Bottom

As we embark on the final stretch of our journey home, the refrain of that song should be our prayer: "Hold thou my hand . . ." God may be holding your spouse's hand, but that's not your hand. He may be holding your father's hand, your mother's hand, your brother's hand, your sister's hand, your best friend's hand; but that's not *your* hand. You need Him to hold *your* hand. I need Him to hold *my* hand. For in the present crisis, we cannot possibly manage on our own.

In chapter 1 I called attention to the legendary Odysseus and his perilous journey home. According to Homer's account, Odysseus, as he approached the region of the sirens, was fully aware of their wickedly enchanting music and of the fate of sailors who, succumbing to their bewitchment, had gone ashore to their ruin. Only by having himself strapped securely to the mast of his ship (with his men under strict orders not to let him loose, regardless of his pleadings or commands) could he himself endure unscathed the haunting, mesmerizing enticement of these treacherous minstrels.

A host of similar perils lie strewn along the journey to our heavenly home. Like the legendary sirens, the world beckons. Worldly customs and practices keep encroaching. And some Christians, ignoring Scripture and all sensible precedents, are pushing the envelope as far as it will go. Worldly dancing and drinking, for example, are creeping into Adventist weddings, family celebrations, and other functions. A pastor friend told me a while back that he and his wife were handed a drink as they arrived at a wedding reception, in which the groom was a high official of an Adventist institution. Noticing suspicious bubbles in their glasses, they learned, upon inquiry, that it was, indeed (as they say), the "real thing." Handing it back, they requested something virgin, a request that took about 10 minutes to fill—as if those in charge needed to execute a search for the scarce commodity!

The reception was filled with other Adventists who apparently made no similar request.

Moreover, it was a Sabbath afternoon, my friend said, and as soon as the sun went down, the pace and tone of the music picked up, and the couple, joined by others, took to the floor.

Cases like that are no longer as isolated as they used to be. Recently someone shared with me a copy of an invitation to a birthday party for an Adventist friend. It read, "Join us for an evening of fun and dancing."

A never-ending barrage of sleek advertising in the public media seems to be having its effect—the funny ones, especially. Prepared by wickedly gifted individuals, masters in human psychology and manipulation, such ads get us first to laugh, then to sing their jingle, then finally, in the near or distant future when the chips are down, to grab a glass and "sample" the product.

And there are issues all across the entertainment spectrum today. Just to mention movies and similar activities for a split second, I find it ironic that what I would call Adventist movie prohibition came in what might now be seen as the good old days. For what was showing then is Sunday school stuff compared to the hard-core offerings of today. Which means that our "liberation" has come at a time when such entertainment is characterized by unimaginable violence, incredible vulgarity, and the most reprehensible prurience.

I point to these activities, not because they are the most serious lapses in the church today, but because, like canaries in a coal mine, they can serve as warnings of more serious danger ahead or already here. I point to them because they represent perhaps the first visible wave of assault from the secular culture all around us. If we find Adventists becoming a regular part of the nightclub scene (as is the case in some circles), then we can know that we are facing issues that transcend the act itself.

The enticements and allurements confronting contemporary Christians are truly breathtaking, hitting us from all directions. Like Siren songs, they invite us to turn aside, to sample, to taste, to indulge. Our only safety, as was Odysseus', is to be "tied" to the mast of the ship. And that mast is the cross of Jesus. Paul's strong plea is relevant here: "With eyes wide open to the mercies of God," he said, "I beg you, my brothers, as an act of intelligent worship, to give him your bodies, as a living sacrifice, consecrated to him. . . . Don't let the world around you squeeze you into its own mould, but let God re-mould your minds from within" (Rom. 12:1, 2, Phillips).

Beyond the encroaching worldliness, one of the deadliest perils we face, and one that affects more areas of people's lives than they care to recognize, is scientism, a movement that's been gaining momentum ever since the Enlightenment of the seventeenth century; picking up steam in the middle of the nineteenth through the work and influence of people such as Charles Darwin; and now is bearing down upon this generation like a giant, mythological bulldozer, leveling everything in its path. Its aim is nothing less than the complete displacement of God as a working hypothesis in human thought and behavior, the dismantling of religion, and the establishment of science as the god for our times.

It's the ultimate idolatry. But in the wake of contemporary scientific and technological wonders that verily stagger the imagination, it becomes terribly easy to fall down before this new god and worship it. And the human heart loves a god like that because, like Rachel's gods, it's a god we can sit on, a god that makes no moral demands. And what we're seeing today is that areas of morality and behavior that used to be clear and unambiguous are no longer so, with even men and women of the cloth giving the trumpet a most uncertain sound.

No less a figure than the former archbishop of Canterbury Rowan Williams argues, for example, that "the absolute condemnation of same-sex relations of intimacy [relies] . . . on an abstract fundamentalist deployment of a number of very ambiguous texts"[3] And widely acclaimed evangelical speaker Tony Campolo, in a May 2007 appearance on national television in the United States, informed the public that his wife (unlike himself) "is a strong advocate for gay marriage."[4]

What I didn't know as I listened to that program was that advocates such as Mrs. Campolo represented only the tip of a huge iceberg headed our way. Six or seven years later the entire moral ground is shifting under us, with certain established biblical standards and principles widely perceived as having gone way past their cultural shelf life. But to borrow a statement from writer Cullen Murphy, "Changes that seem inconsequential over a single lifetime can upend the social order over three or four."[5] While I was attending an international congress on preaching in Cambridge, England, some years ago, an insightful comment from one participant caught my attention. "Our generation," he said, "is coping with issues our parents never had nightmares about."

It's getting worse. And Adventists must be prepared for it. "When the religion of Christ is most held in contempt," said Ellen G. White, "when His law is most despised, then should our zeal be the warmest and our courage and firmness the most unflinching. To stand in defense of truth and righteousness when the majority forsake us, to fight the battles of the Lord when champions are few—this will be our test. At this time we must gather warmth from the coldness of others, courage from their cowardice, and loyalty from their treason."[6]

The basic point of this chapter's title is that as we come down to the close of time, the moral and spiritual situation in the world and in the church will become so utterly confusing, so polarized, so chaotic, that those who'd be faithful to God may find themselves unable (unlike Joshua) to count even on the support of their own "household." A time when, as they say in some parts of the Caribbean, *every tub must sit on its own bottom*, meaning that each person will have to be accountable for their own destiny.

When Joshua said, "As for me and my household," he was retreating to the smallest community unit, the family—in case the larger Israelite community should abandon their loyalty to Yahweh. But the point of this chapter is that the times are becoming critical, dangerous, ugly. And the day is perhaps not far off when, instead of saying, as did Joshua, "But as for me *and my household*," we may only be able to say, "But as for me."

Others, including my own family, may decide to embrace the god of science and technology, with its glowing, mesmerizing promise of a brave new world for everyone; but as for me . . .

Others, including my own family, may turn their back on the Sabbath, caught up in the contemporary rat race and the intoxicating consumerism of our times; but as for me . . .

Others, including my own family, may decide that the pleasures of this world are more attractive, more captivating, than the things of God; that this church of ours is too straitlaced, too narrow-minded, too strict, too meddlesome, too backward, too yesterday; but as for me . . .

Others, including my own family, may abandon the church—that mysterious entity Jesus founded upon the rock of His own power. And they may even do it for humanly logical and rational reasons, having come up against the blatant injustice and hypocrisy of "the brethren"; but I, for one, have decided long ago to let no saint or miscreant drive me from my heavenly Father's house and am prepared, against all odds, to say, by the grace of God, "Others may leave, but as for me . . .

Others, including my own family, may turn their backs on Jesus, *but as for me, I choose Him!* For by faith I look back to one dark Friday 2,000 years ago to a figure on a cross outside old Jerusalem and watch as the awesome burden of the sin of ages strangles His soul. There's a statement in Hebrews 2:9 that Jesus, "by the grace of God," tasted death for everyone. But one New Testament scholar recently called attention to a startling variant found in a few of the very earliest manuscripts. Instead of saying that Jesus, "by the grace of God," tasted death for everyone, these earliest manuscripts say that Jesus, "without God," tasted death for everyone.

If this is correct, it helps us understand a little better Jesus' cry of utter abandonment on the cross that dark Friday afternoon: "Eli, Eli, lema sabachthani? . . . My God, my God, why have you forsaken me?" (Matt. 27:46). *Jesus was dying without God, utterly alone*—for you and for me.

And the one gift I want to give to Him is my life—myself, so that on that coming day He might see "the travail of His soul" and be satisfied that at least for me His death has made an eternal difference. And whether I die first or remain alive, I look forward to hearing one day that trumpet blast from heaven that wakes the dead and in one split second transforms the living into a state of glorious immortality.

Hallelujah!

---

[1] Roy Adams, *Crossing Jordan: Joshua, Holy War, and God's Unfailing Promises* (Hagerstown, Md.: Review and Herald Pub. Assn., 2005).

[2] Maria Puente, "The Sweet Smell of Excess," *USA Today*, Feb. 4, 2005, http://usatoday30.usatoday.com/life/people/2005-02-03-celeb-auctions_x.htm.

[3] Cited in Rupert Shortt, *Rowan Williams: An Introduction* (Harrisburg, Pa.: Morehouse Pub., 2003), p. 51.

[4] "Falwell Blazed Trail in American Politics, Religious Right," interview, May 15, 2007, *PBS Newshour*, http://www.pbs.org/newshour/bb/remember/jan-june07/falwell_05-15.html.

[5] C. Murphy, *Are We Rome?* p. 21.

[6] E. G. White, *Testimonies*, vol. 5, p. 136.

Chapter 18

Looking for a City: The Quest That Burns in Every Christian Heart

"We have an altar from which those who serve the tabernacle have no right to eat. For the bodies of those animals, whose blood is brought into the sanctuary by the high priest for sin, are burned outside the camp. Therefore Jesus also, that He might sanctify the people with His own blood, suffered outside the gate. Therefore let us go forth to Him, outside the camp, bearing His reproach. For here we have no continuing city, but we seek the one to come" (Heb. 13:10-14, NKJV).

For decades I've been fascinated by this cryptic passage. But for a long time, its first lines stumped me. I found them dense, heavy, utterly remote from our times. Yet I couldn't escape the fact that both logically and theologically, the author saw them as the anchor for his point.

So what do those lines mean? What is this "altar" mentioned in verse 10? Who are referred to as "those who serve the tabernacle"? What tabernacle is this? And why would those who serve it "have no right to eat" from the altar in question? What is verse 11 talking about when it mentions the bodies of animals being "burned outside the camp"?

I discovered that that last detail harks back to a seemingly obscure ritual on the ancient Day of Atonement, found in Leviticus 16:27: "The bull and the goat for the sin offerings, whose blood was brought into the Most Holy Place to make atonement, must be taken outside the camp; their hides, flesh and offal are to be burned up."

The Leviticus text in no way indicates that the ritual in question pointed to anything beyond itself. But now the author of Hebrews, in a letter filled with ancient sanctuary allusions, zeros in on that particular symbolism to make an enormously important theological point to his readers as he winds down his famous letter. That Atonement Day ritual, he says in effect, pointed forward to the Messiah's death.

But in making that point, he does not emphasize the aspect of burning but rather its *location*—namely, "outside the gate." That detail hardly resonates with twenty-first-century readers, for whom city walls and gates are relics of a distant past. But the apostle's first-century readers would have caught his drift immediately. For them, "outside the camp" (or "outside the gate") was "an unclean place, a place of separation and death, where lepers roamed, criminals were executed, and the bodies used for sin offerings were burned (see Lev. 13:46; 24:14; Deut. 23:14)."[1]

It was an in-your-face argument for the apostle's first audience, almost universally believed to be Christian Jews living in Rome, the capital of the empire, and under heavy pressure to abandon their faith in Jesus. In the wake of enormous social, psychological, and physical tension, they faced the temptation to return to Judaism, the religion of their ancestors, still comparatively well respected in the famous capital.

Confronting the problem head-on, the apostle flatly says, in effect: "Those ceremonies and rituals to which you're tempted to return have been made theologically irrelevant by the death of Jesus. Christians have a new altar, a cosmic altar, from which those still doing animal sacrifices in Jerusalem have 'no right to eat' " (see Heb. 13:10). And verses 11 and 12 drive home the point that some 30 years earlier, as Jesus bowed in death on a Friday afternoon outside Jerusalem ("outside the gate"), something epochal had transpired. As the veil of the Temple mysteriously ripped in two, exposing the Most Holy Place to public view, it was an indication that the old system had suddenly become outmoded, with the theological focus shifting to a celestial altar, where Jesus, our Great High Priest, ministers in the presence of God.

By the manner of His death—"outside the gate"—Jesus had become a curse for us, in fulfillment of the ancient ritual. He'd borne our shame. "Therefore," says the apostle, clinching his fundamental point, "let us go forth to Him, outside the camp, bearing His reproach" (verse 13).

And reproach it was indeed. Jesus was not popular in first-century Rome. Roman sophisticates saw Christianity as a religion of slaves and nincompoops. An ancient graffiti, now in the Palatine Museum in Rome, depicts a slave named Alexamenos kneeling before a cross. On the cross is the figure of man with the head of a donkey, the mocking caption reading, "Alexamenos worships [his] God."[2]

In the Roman capital, Christianity was regarded as a stupidity, a creed for idiots. But it was precisely in that context that the apostle's appeal received its poignancy: "Therefore let us go forth to Him, outside the camp, bearing His reproach."

We Face a Similar Pressure

Christianity is not popular in the twenty-first century either. Assaults upon our faith are coming good and plenty from every direction—more subtle, perhaps, but just as potent. Take as a random example *The Da Vinci Code* of 2003.[3] The novel, and the movie based on it, took the world by storm, with millions of people getting their first read about Christianity through a fictional work designed to portray the idea of Jesus' divinity as a concoction of the Catholic Church.

Four years later came *The Lost Tomb of Jesus.* Viewed by millions on the Discovery channel, the 2007 documentary by Simcha Jacobovici claimed that the remains of Jesus and Mary Magdalene had been discovered in a tomb in Jerusalem. The sensational "find" grabbed a Western media hungry for scandal and was yet another effort to kill faith in Jesus, to present Christianity as a hoax. Prove you have the bones of Jesus, and Christianity is dead!

For not a few modern intellectuals, Christians are empty-headed numskulls. But like their first-century Roman counterparts, modern Christians must "go forth to [Jesus], outside the camp, bearing His reproach."

This has always been the lot of those who follow the Lord. In Hebrews 11 the apostle spoke of those who'd been "tortured" for their witness to God, those who'd been mocked, scourged, and imprisoned for their faith in God. "They were stoned," he said, "sawn in two, . . . slain with the sword. They wandered about in sheepskins and goatskins, being destitute, afflicted, tormented. . . . They wandered in deserts and mountains, in dens and caves of the earth" (verses 35-38, NKJV).

What gave them strength to submit to such abuse? And what will impel us to do the same today? The answer comes in the famous sentence to which the author had been building all along: "For here we have no continuing city, but we seek the one to come" (Heb. 13:14, NKJV).

Seeing Beyond the Present

I can imagine that last line being read on Sabbath morning at a house church that meets in an affluent section of Rome. And I can imagine some wealthy sophisticate looking out the window at the capital of the great Roman Empire and wondering what madman or madwoman could envision an end of that great city.

After all, Rome showed every sign of living up to its description as "the eternal city." The "mistress of the Mediterranean world," all the surrounding countries lay at her feet, her trade and commerce dominating the entire region and beyond. The Roman poet Claudian boasted that "Heaven could show nothing fairer; that no eye could see her immensity, no heart feel all her beauty, no tongue sing all her praise."[4] And Callinicus of Petra compared the deprivation of those who had not seen Rome to that of blind persons who do not know the sun. Only the person who knows Rome, he said, could dare say that he or she has lived.[5] When the Caesars marched, the entire Mediterranean and all of Asia trembled.

But Rome fell! "Here have we no continuing city."

It's not an easy lesson to learn. In every generation the tendency has been to think that the structures and institutions we've created will last forever. And perhaps ours is the easiest generation in which to become enamored with our scientific and technological wizardry.

James Gleick's book *Faster*[6] gives a series of hair-raising examples of some of the technological wonders of our times in the areas of time and speed. We used to talk about the "split second," meaning an extremely short time. Then came the millisecond, one thousandth of a second, and we used to think, *Wow! That's short! That's quick!* But here in this book I began to read about the *nanosecond*—one billionth of a second!

And just when you thought we'd arrived at the ultimate in quickness, you learn that we're now down to the *femtosecond*—one millionth of a nanosecond!

I had to read that several times. It just about blew my mind to realize that such infinitesimally minuscule time measurements are not simply theoretical constructs but actually are being utilized in the pinpoint accuracy needed for the functioning of certain precision technology operations, such as global positioning systems (GPS) and guided missile technology.

Wow!

The danger, however, is that the present with its glamour, its scientific and technological wizardry, its materialistic sophistication, its brilliance, its dazzle, and its neon flashing can hypnotize us. It can spook us into forgetting the fundamental transitoriness of human life, the ephemeralness of human civilization, however advanced or sophisticated.

But perhaps the modern phenomenon that keeps millions bedazzled and awestruck by the present culture is the entertainment industry, especially as exhibited in Hollywood and on its satellites. Think of the endless award ceremonies and the international attention they command. Today we have the Oscar, the Emmy, the Grammy, the Tony, the Golden Globe, the American Music, the Country Music, the People's Choice, the Screen Actors Guild, the Nickelodeon, and a host of others. *Variety* counted more than 565 such trophies and award ceremonies in 2000.

And to each of these events and ceremonies the stars come out in all their dazzling glory, while the rest of us sit at home enamored by the ostentation and the glamour, in comparison to what we often perceive as our dull, boring, pedestrian lives. In the words of Chris Hedges: "The American oligarchy, 1 percent of whom control more wealth than the bottom 90 percent combined, are the characters we envy and watch on television. They live and play in multimillion-dollar beach houses and expansive modern lofts. They marry professional athletes and are chauffeured in stretch limos to spa appointments. They rush from fashion shows to movie premieres, flaunting their surgically enhanced, perfect bodies in haute couture. Their teenagers throw $200,000 parties and have $1 million weddings. This life is held before us like a beacon."[7]

The ancient psalmist was puzzled by "the ungodly, who prosper in the world," who "increase in riches" (Ps. 73:12, KJV), whose gaudy images adorn the pages of the Internet every day—whether they're getting married or divorcing or shacking up or cavorting on their multimillion-dollar yachts. It's as if glamour and conspicious wealth constituted the newly discovered way to security, happiness, and immortality—as if all my righteous living were in vain. "When I tried to understand all this," the psalmist said, "it troubled me deeply till I entered the sanctuary of God; then I understood their final destiny" (verses 16, 17, NIV).

How true! That massive white HOLLYWOOD sign in Los Angeles actually looks down on the place where many of the Hollywood luminaries end up—the Hollywood Forever Cemetery, with its "faux Italian Renaissance marble buildings, [with] rows of crypts" containing the remains of dead celebrities, and "huge marble monuments to the wealthy and the powerful." "Tourists are promised 'visits' with dead stars, who are referred to as 'residents.'" The cemetery is "divided into sections with names like Garden of Eternal Love and Garden of Legends."[8]

Everything to mask the cruel reality of death; everything to deny the hard-nosed fact that "here we do not have an enduring city."

Switching channels one Saturday evening some years ago, I came across a rebroadcast of an old MGM anniversary documentary that featured a star-studded gathering in a huge makeshift restaurant created for the occasion and billed as the largest restaurant in history, if only for one night. Anybody who was anybody in Hollywood musicals was there: Fred Astaire, Bing Crosby, Red Skelton, Judy Garland, Eleanor Powell, Nelson Eddy, etc. At least 500 stars must have been present for the gathering, the camera panning in on row after row of them, each one playing up to it and strutting their stuff as only movie stars can do.

But as I looked into the faces of the vast array of celebrities, the thought suddenly struck me: *They're all dead now, every last one of them!*

The message is crystal clear: As with nations and civilizations, so with individuals—however glamorous or wealthy or powerful. "Here we do not have an enduring city."

Seeking a Better Place

It's not enough simply to believe that the world as we know it will not last forever. Even nonreligious people are coming around to acknowledging that, however darkly. The final week of 2006 was dubbed Armageddon Week on the History Channel in the United States; and on December 26 the channel ran a program entitled *Last Days on Earth*, depicting what they called "the seven deadliest threats to humanity."

One to two hundred years ago, one astrophysicist on the program intoned, textbooks presented the universe as a peaceful, gentle place. But "we have come to learn," he said, "that the universe has no shortage of ways it can kill us." An asteroid (the program said), for example, could wipe us out. A flu pandemic could depopulate the planet. A star could collapse, producing gamma rays, "radioactive light brighter than a million trillion suns," killing all of us. Black holes, long thought to be stationary, are now believed to be moving at thousands of miles per hour—invisible "cosmic vacuum cleaners" that can suck in our entire planet like a speck of dust.

Yes, others besides Christians anticipate an end to human civilization. But darkness pervades every vision of the future they articulate. By contrast, Scripture affirms that "we have no continuing city [here], *but we seek the one to come.*" And ahead of us is a long line of pilgrims who've taken up this journey to that celestial place. Chapter 11 of Hebrews, "the Westminster Abbey of the Bible," contains a partial list of these heaven-bound travelers. Among them the patriarch Abraham, who, it says, "was looking forward to the city with foundations, whose architect and builder is God" (verse 10).

"Pie in the sky," some scoffers call it. Wishful thinking. Diagnosed in 1963 with a degenerative disease doctors thought would end his life within a few years, the world-famous 72-year-old Cambridge physicist and cosmologist, Stephen Hawking, spoke to the (London) *Guardian* back in May 2011. Having "lived with the prospect of an early death for the last 49 years," he said, "I'm not afraid of death. . . . I regard the brain as a computer which will stop working when its components fail. There is no heaven or afterlife for broken down computers; that is a fairy story for people afraid of the dark."[9]

But heaven is a bedrock promise of Scripture, not for "people afraid of the dark," but for people who refuse to get used to the darkness of this wicked planet and its endless sea of grief and pain and hurt, for people who share Abraham's yearning for a better place.

A poem I learned back in elementary school brings it home. Written by the British writer Felicia Hemans (1793-1835), against the bleak background of England's Victorian period (described so devastatingly in the writings of Charles Dickens), it depicts, as I imagine it, a conversation between a young boy and his poverty-stricken Christian mother; the young boy is already tired of the abject misery all around him and yearning for the fulfillment of his mother's fondest dreams:

"I hear thee speak of the Better Land,
Thou call'st its children a happy band;
Mother, oh! where is that radiant shore?
Shall we not seek it, and weep no more?
Is it where the flower of the orange blows,
And the fire-flies glance through the myrtle boughs?"
"Not there, not there, my child!"

"Is it where the feathery palm-trees rise,
And the date grows ripe under sunny skies?
Or 'midst the green islands of glittering seas,
Where fragrant forests perfume the breeze,
And strange bright birds, on their starry wings,
Bear the rich hues of all glorious things?"
"Not there, not there, my child!"

"Is it far away, in some region old,
Where the rivers wander o'er sands of gold;

Where the burning rays of the ruby shine,
And the diamond lights up the secret mine,
And the pearl gleams forth from the coral strand;
Is it there, sweet mother, that Better Land?"
"Not there, not there, my child!—

"Eye hath not seen it, my gentle boy;
Ear hath not heard its deep songs of joy;
Dreams cannot picture a world so fair:
Sorrow and death may not enter there;
Time doth not breathe on its fadeless bloom;
For beyond the clouds and beyond the tomb—
It is there, it is there, my child!"[10]

And there's where our fondest hope should find its anchor. "For here we do not have an enduring city, but we are looking for the city that is to come."

---

[1] William G. Johnsson, *Hebrews: Full Assurance for Christians Today* (Boise, Idaho: Pacific Press Pub. Assn., 1994), p. 339.

[2] James Grout, "Rome: The Home of Empire and of All Perfection, Alexamenos Graffito, *Encyclopaedia Romana* (University of Chicago, 2013), http://penelope.uchicago.edu/~grout/encyclopaedia_romana/gladiators/graffito.html.

[3] Dan Brown, *The Da Vinci Code* (New York: Doubleday/Random House, 2003).

[4] Ludwig Friedläender, *Roman Life and Manners Under the Early Empire* (New York: E. P. Dutton, 1908), p. 6.

[5] *Ibid.*

[6] James Gleick, *Faster: The Acceleration of Just About Everything* (New York: Pantheon Books, 1999).

[7] Chris Hedges, *Empire of Illusion: The End of Literacy and the Triumph of Spectacle* (New York: Nation Books, 2009), p. 26.

[8] *Ibid.*, p. 18.

[9] "Stephen Hawking: 'There Is No Heaven; It's a Fairy Story,'" interview by Ian Sample, *The Guardian*, May 15, 2011, http://www.guardian.co.uk/science/2011/may/15/stephen-hawking-interview-there-is-no-heaven.

[10] *Royal Readers*, no. 3, first series (London: T. Nelson and Sons, Ltd., 1935), pp. 73, 74.